# TO BE FRANK

## EVERYTHING YOU NEED TO KNOW ABOUT DOG BEHAVIOUR

AFTAB AHMED

Approved by Frank

First published 2023
by Rowanvale Books Ltd
The Gate
Keppoch Street
Roath
Cardiff
CF24 3JW
www.rowanvalebooks.com

A CIP catalogue record for this book is available from the British Library.

ISBN: 978-1-914422-80-5
eBook ISBN: 978-1-914422-79-9

Dear Diane

Hope you get a little
time to read this
I think you'll like it.

Aftab
x

# CONTENTS

# INTRODUCTION

My interest in wildlife programmes and empathy for the plight of animals piqued my interest in animal behaviour from an early age. My thirst for knowledge of all things dog started in earnest in early 1990 and led to me qualifying as a dog behaviourist. I initially trained with the *Cambridge Institute of Dog Training and Behaviour* and then the *International School for Canine Psychology and Behaviour*, the *Institute of Modern Dog Trainers*, and the *International Association of Animal Behavior Consultants* to become a certified dog behaviour consultant.

As a dog behaviourist, I have been fortunate to have worked with most dog breeds, ranging from Chihuahuas and dachshunds to Great Danes, Dobermans and German shepherds, and have been able to help clients with virtually all unwanted behaviours exhibited by their dogs.

## BEFORE THE DOG YEARS

I wish I could tell you that I've always loved dogs and have had a lifelong affinity with them. Unfortunately, I can't.

As a child, I must confess that I didn't really care much for dogs. I might go so far as to say that I was nervous around them.

My earliest memories of dogs are limited and certainly nothing that inclined me towards owning one. These memories include jumping out of my skin on passing someone's front garden and being confronted by a lunging dog intent on tearing me apart – thank goodness it was chained and yanked to a halt a metre away from me. Another abiding memory is of a friend's dachshund that would happily have had your finger if you went within ten paces of him. Whenever he growled, my friend's father would smack him on the snout. Alternatively, the dachshund would alight on my friend's father's lap and give me the evil eye for the duration of my stay. So, no great, positive, life-changing experiences that got a dog onto any of my wish lists.

It wasn't until 1994, when my son Remi, aged four, and daughter Natasha, aged two, supported by an irksome au pair, persuaded us to buy our first dog. I say 'us', but the truth of the matter is that my wife would have been quite happy to restrict our animal care obligations to a solitary budgerigar. However, the au pair promised she would be responsible for dog care including walks, feeding, etc. So, along came a German short-haired pointer, who we named Cato.

Of course, I thought I knew everything I needed to know about dogs by then – based solely on a diet of Barbara Woodhouse. Remember her? She used to terrify not only the dogs but their owners during her very popular TV series in the 1980s. Her advice was binary: praise your dog when he listens to you, and tell him off when he doesn't! Easy-peasy.

Dear Barbara never really explained what to do if the dog didn't listen even after he had been told off, or at least I don't remember any such advice. What were we supposed to do with our beautiful young puppy who was incessantly biting us with his needle-sharp teeth? Not satisfied with human flesh, he further honed his skills on furniture and clothes! As responsible dog owners, we called in a local dog trainer. She was well regarded. She'd written a book. She was obviously a professional. 'Smack him on the snout, hold him by the scruff of the neck and give him a jolly good shake whilst simultaneously giving him a stern look.' If that didn't work, we were advised to put Tabasco sauce or lemon on our fingers and anything else the puppy had a fondness for chewing.

My wallet had been unburdened of £30, but my conscience had been burdened by doubt and guilt. Something told me this couldn't be the way forward. I don't know what that something was. Maybe it was common sense. After all, I wouldn't do that to a baby if it bit me.

I wondered and worried about the impact on Cato of being told off and, for example, shaken by the scruff of the neck if he nipped me. In my research, I came across many 'experts' advocating shouting, squirting water, or making loud noises to deter unwanted behaviours and generally using intimidating tactics to 'train' dogs.

Oh, and incidentally, the local trainer's advice didn't really work.

# WHO'S THIS BOOK FOR?

In this book, I share everything that I have learned about dogs over the past 20 years. This includes effective methods and strategies that will work in modifying behaviour. I also share strategies you should avoid, either because they won't work or, worse still, will lead you down the road to perdition and cause more harm than good. Real case studies are included to emphasise the effectiveness of different strategies.

This book will help you understand why dogs display certain behaviours. Why are some dogs aggressive and others not? What are dogs telling us in their language, the intricacies of which are often unclear to us? And how can we get our dogs to listen to us? In this book, I'll explain why being forceful is not the best way to get a dog to listen, and why kinder methods are the best way forward in training a dog and modifying problem behaviours.

Both shiny new dog owners and not-so-shiny old hacks will find this book useful in increasing their knowledge on what really makes dogs tick.

Along the way, I'll dispel some common myths about dogs and explain why some behaviours that seem rather odd or inexplicable to us are perfectly normal and understandable when viewed from a dog's perspective.

Finally, if your dog does display undesirable behaviours that are causing distress to you, others or the dog himself, then in this book you'll find advice and guidance on **how to modify those unwanted behaviours using kind, reward-based techniques**. The advice and methods set out in this book are based on science and experience. For each behaviour, I explain the reason behind the behaviour, how best to stop it, and how to change it to a far more desirable behaviour. Crucially, the methods are effective.

Some of these problematic behaviours became particularly prevalent due to the Covid pandemic lockdown in 2020: separation-related disorders, dog aggression and general dog nervousness/anxiety.

## SAD STATISTICS

Before lockdown, 30% of dog owners reported that their dogs showed some signs of aggression and 44% said their dogs showed some signs of anxiety or fear.[1] There has not been much research in the UK on separation anxiety specifically, but some research from Cincinnati suggests that 20–40% of dogs are affected by this. Of course, there may be some overlap here with the 44% showing 'anxiety and fear' in Bekoff's research.

Research published in late December 2020, supported fears that changes in our behaviour during lockdown, including fewer opportunities to go out for dog walks and spending little time away from our dogs, affected the behaviour of our pooches, including a substantial increase in anxiety and clinginess.[2] Significantly, there was a 40% increase in Google searches for 'dog bite'. Because of this, I've made sure to give particular attention in this book to the reasons behind aggressive behaviours towards people, leash reactivity and separation-related behaviours.

For altruistic reasons, I wish it were a requirement to attend a course on dog ownership before owning a dog. That might help reduce some other shocking statistics. For example, in 2022, 664,000 dogs were left at UK shelters.[3] A large proportion of these 664,000 dogs were surrendered because of behavioural problems.

Many of these dogs just don't find homes. 80,000 dogs are euthanised each year. A third of all canine euthanisations in the UK are dogs under the age of three years who displayed 'undesirable' behaviours.[4] This last statistic is particularly sad, as most behavioural problems are preventable and resolvable.

If you like dogs and want to offer them the best life possible, this book is for you.

---

1      Bekoff, M. (2019) 'Demographics and Links Among Behavior Problems in Dogs.' *Psychology Today*. Available from https://www.psychologytoday.com/gb/blog/animal-emotions/201905/demographics-and-links-among-behavior-problems-in-dogs. [Accessed on 7th April 2022]

2      Christley, R., Murray, J. K., et al. (2020) 'Impact of the First COVID-19 Lockdown on Management of Pet Dogs in the UK.' *Animals*, vol. 11(1):5 DOI:10.3390/ani11010005

3      Cosgrove, N. (2022) '12 UK Animal Shelter Statistics & Facts to Know in 2022: Benefits, Facts & More.' *PetKeen*. Available from https://petkeen.com/animal-shelter-statistics-uk/#:~:text=The%2012%20Most%20Shocking%20UK,are%20not%20spayed%20or%20neutered. [Accessed on 15th April 2022]

4      Boyd, C., Jarvis, S., et al. (2018), 'Mortality resulting from undesirable behaviours in dogs aged under three years attending primary-care veterinary practices in England.' *Animal Welfare* (2018). DOI: 10.7120/09627286.27.3.251

# QUIZ

Try the fun quiz below. No googling! Do you know more than your partner? Answers are on page 201. May the best man/woman win – and no cheating!

**1. Play-biting among puppies and in relation to humans:**
- Is an unnatural behaviour that is unacceptable.
- Is a natural behaviour that helps to establish bite inhibition – a sense of how hard they can bite without causing injury.
- Always stops of its own accord as the dog matures.
- Should be encouraged to develop a strong character.

**2. The main cause of separation anxiety is:**
- When a puppy/dog gets excessive attention or has not been conditioned to an appropriate routine.
- Breed predisposition.
- Lack of obedience training.
- The house in which the dog resides being too big.

**3. What are the three main reasons for destructive behaviour?**
- Attention seeking, fun and exercise.
- Breed predisposition, over-excitement and exercise.
- Normal puppy behaviour, boredom and separation anxiety.
- Resentment, onset of gum disease and monotony.

**4. If your dog is whining because of separation anxiety, you should:**
- Ignore him.
- Reprimand him and then praise him when he's quiet.
- Help him understand that there's nothing to be anxious about.
- Put some calming music on to distract him.

**5. If your dog stops to say hello to another dog when you're training him to walk to heel, you should:**
- Stop when the dog stops, thereby keeping the leash loose.
- Stop, as otherwise you are preventing the dog from exploring.
- Reprimand the dog as a demonstration of your leadership.
- Continue walking.

**6. It is recommended that you do not allow a puppy to lick people's faces because:**
- It is a serious risk to human health.
- It is established that this can lead to obsessive-compulsive behaviours.
- It may cause separation related problems.
- It may encourage jumping up as the dog matures.

**7. When a dog solicits attention from you through pawing, jumping up and such like, you should NOT:**
- Ignore the dog by avoiding eye contact, touch and voice acknowledgement.
- Stand up to prevent the dog jumping on to your lap.
- Push the dog off.
- Move to another area of the house.

**8. Praise and rewards should occur:**
- Within ten seconds of the dog's action.
- Within a minute or so.
- Within two seconds of the dog's action.
- Within 20 seconds of the dog's action.

**9. What is the most sensitive socialisation period of a dog's life?**
- 1–8 weeks.
- 5–16 weeks.
- 12–20 weeks.
- 16–24 weeks.

**10. If a dog barks excessively for your attention when alone in a room, you should:**

- Wait ten minutes before entering the room.
- Wait for a gap in the barking before entering the room.
- Open the door quickly and throw the dog some food.
- Wait outside the room and reassure the dog with a soft voice.

# CHAPTER 1 – WHAT IS BEHAVIOUR?

Some dog behaviours are adorable. Nothing perks me up more than seeing my daughter's cockapoo, Frank, sauntering over from his bed (or my wife's lap), gracing me with his presence and asking for a calming belly rub. There's no mistaking this invitation. He nudges me with his head, flops to his side and then rolls over enthusiastically onto his back, legs akimbo with wrists relaxed and floppy.

Then there are the behaviours on which I am normally consulted by clients. Behaviours which people find unpleasant, unwanted and unacceptable. When a dog bites a child, it's not so adorable.

Since this book is all about dog behaviours, particularly those that are undesirable from our perspective, this chapter covers the basic principles of behaviours and their purposes.

I like Dr Susan G Friedman, a professor at Utah State University who pioneered the idea of Applied Behaviour Analysis. Specifically,

I like the way she gets people thinking about the concept of behaviour. So, as a sincere form of flattery, I do the same with my clients. Thanks, Susan.

At seminars or during one-to-one consultations, I often ask, "What are legs and what is their purpose?" I might also ask the same thing about eyes, ears, hands and so on. The answers to these questions are always readily forthcoming, clear and concise, and met with general universal approval amongst the audience, evidenced by much head nodding. However, when I then ask the same hitherto enlightened audience, "What is behaviour and what is its purpose?", the response is comparatively muted, variable and often accompanied by much head scratching.

To help you avoid ever being caught with an itchy head, here's the lowdown on behaviour and the seven most important things you need to know.

**First**, dog behaviour is simply a form of communication that we typically experience with our eyes and ears. A dog barks, we hear it. A dog cowers or wags his tail, we see it. Hopefully you will never experience a particularly painful behaviour involving your sense of touch. A bite is not an experience I would wish on anyone. After reading this book, and especially taking Chapters 6 and 10 on board, it is unlikely that you will ever be bitten.

The **second** thing you should understand about behaviour, is its purpose: the dog's behaviour is intended to gain a valuable outcome from the environment or to avoid a situation.

Gaining a valuable outcome for a dog is all about access to something that he enjoys. It could be access to a resource: for example, a toy or food. It could be access to an activity: "C'mon, Mum, let's get to the park or my mate Barney!" Of course, it could also be about access to your attention. Nothing short of physical restraint can keep a dog from running to you when you come downstairs first thing in the morning or when you return home from a day in the office or a trip to the shops. When it comes to gaining access, the dog wants to reduce the distance between himself and the resource.

On the other hand, when avoiding a situation, it is the dog's intention to create distance between the situation and himself. Avoidance is all about escape, and normally occurs when the dog is faced with a situation that is unpleasant for him. Escape communication/ behaviour for a dog is normally expressed through running away, submission or aggression. If your dog sees a tractor and it frightens him, he'll either run away, cower (often behind your legs) or bark aggressively.

*"No thanks."*

*"Go away or else…"*

The **third** thing about behaviours is that they meet the dog's needs and will only continue if they work. If they didn't work to meet the dog's needs, they would be functionless and the dog simply wouldn't bother continuing to use those behaviours.

**Fourthly**, most behaviours are learned, but there are also those that could be termed 'automatic'. These are behaviours that are not socially maintained or contingent on what's going on in the dog's environment. Automatic behaviours include a dog drooling when he sees his favourite titbit and you're being far too slow in handing it over. Or a startle reflex following a loud noise. Or cocking his leg to pee.

**Fifthly**, as we will discuss in Chapter 3, emotions and arousal levels of dogs are major factors that drive behaviours. Additionally, a variety of other factors can influence and drive behaviour, such as health issues, genetic predisposition, biochemical factors and hormonal levels.

**Sixthly**, unless you're well-versed in understanding a dog's body language and all the sounds that might emanate from him, it's not always easy to know what the intended purpose of any given behaviour is. As a simple example, it's not always easy to know what a dog means when he barks. Does he want you to go away? Is he stressed? Is he scared? Does he want your attention? Does he want a resource? Does he want to access an activity? A bark can convey a whole host of meanings.

The dilemma of meaning is analogous to someone unfamiliar with the English language grappling with the difference between 'through' and 'threw'!

Similarly with body postures, does a 'play bow' convey the same meaning as a 'prey bow'? What does it mean when a dog lowers his head? Is he being submissive or just about to start a chase? All this is discussed in more detail in Chapter 7.

*Is Frank guarding his toy, inviting play or just chilling?*
*Many short-nosed dogs like pugs, bulldogs, etc. (brachycephalic breeds), adopt a position of resting their heads on toys, as demonstrated by Frank in the photograph above, to alleviate breathing problems. So, this position could be a sign of a medical issue in such breeds. My veterinarian colleague Amelia Welham, advises me that owners of dogs that have undergone brachycephalic obstructive airway syndrome surgery (BOAS), often report their sadness to her when their dogs don't sleep with their heads elevated on a toy anymore. Their sadness is soon replaced by joy when they are advised that this was simply their way to avoid suffocation!*

**Here's the final thing about behaviour**. Whilst a particular behaviour might be unacceptable to you, for the dog, it might be perfectly instinctive and normal. As such, is it really a behavioural 'problem'? Or is it just a behaviour that is within the normal range of behaviours for a dog of this age or breed? If it's the latter, then why bother doing anything about it?

Whether you choose do anything about a particular behaviour depends on the impact of it on you and others around you, and your responsibility to give your dog the best life he can have, living harmoniouly with his new human family.

Let's look at a few example behaviours that are very normal, and just need some management in helping the dog understand that other behaviours would be better rewarded.

## SOME SPECIFIC AGE-RELATED BEHAVIOURS PUPPY PHASE (UP TO AROUND 6 MONTHS)

1. **Toileting** – When a puppy arrrives in his new home, he has limited bladder and bowel control and little idea of where he can and can't relieve himself. Added to which, have you seen how much puppies eat?! These three factors mean we, as owners, have to be on top of our game. We need to help him understand, through kind and force-free methods, where he can and can't relieve himself. Conveniently, puppies need to go to the loo like clockwork! Taking them outside just before their time and lavishly praising them when they do go about their business is a surefire way of them repeating it again and again.

2. **Biting** – Being devoid of fingers and thumbs, a puppy will gather a huge amount of information about the environment through his nose and mouth. Our hands, feet, clothes and anything else puppies can get their mouths round – especially if it moves – is fair game and up for exploration.

Again, punishment-based methods to stop a puppy biting, for example hitting, shouting and so on, are not only socially and morally unacceptable, they are unnecessary. Stopping play, looking and acting hurt (you probably *were* hurt, with those needle-sharp teeth!), distracting with a suitable alternative to bite (as you might a child), are far better methods to get the message across to your puppy.

*"Smack him on the nose, shake him by the scruff*
*of his neck and give him a stern look?"*

*"Smack him on the nose, shake him by the scruff*
*of his neck and give him a stern look?"*

# ADOLESCENT PHASE
## (DEPENDING ON THE DOG, THIS IS BETWEEN 6 MONTHS AND 18 MONTHS)

1. **Increased chewing** – At this age, the large molars and jaw muscles are developing. There may be some gum ache, and chewing provides relief. Couple that with the fact that chewing is calming and a de-stresser as it releases endorphins, and your best table and chair legs can easily become fair game.

2. **Unruly behaviour** – If I had £1 every time a client mentioned this term! Hormone levels are elevated during adolescence. The dog will feel a natural need to push boundaries to truly explore new experiences and make his own way in the world. Emotions are easily aroused and 'what I see, I want' syndrome is highly developed. And yet, the thinking part of the brain (prefrontal cortex) is under-developed. This emotional hypersensitivity combined with an immature impulse control system obviously leads to behaviours that are perfectly normal, yet extremely frustrating for owners. Knowing this, you won't be surprised to hear that many dogs are handed into shelters around the age of 12 months for behavioural issues.

Robert Sapolsky reminds us in his book *Behave* that the thinking part of the brain in humans doesn't fully come online until the age of around 25 years (or later, for many people!). Yet we expect so much more of our four-legged friends and expect them to behave perfectly before they're even 12 months old.

*Frank's unruly adolescent behaviour.*

Other than normal, age-related behaviours, there are a host of other 'normal behaviours' that, occasionally, you may choose to do nothing at all about. This is because whether or not a behaviour is undesirable depends on the context and specific circumstances of the owner.

Take for example, **barking**. Even young children know that this is the defining characteristic of a dog. As mentioned earlier, dogs bark for various reasons. Some seem to bark all the time. They see someone, they bark. They see something move, they bark. They see a mate, they bark. Is he expressing his mood, just excited, alerting you to a stranger, or wanting your attention? Now, if you happen to live in a detached house in the country with the nearest neighbour a mile away, or you are slightly hard of hearing, alert barking might be quite desirable. But if you live in a terraced house and your dog alerts you each time someone walks by, it might just get a tad annoying for the neighbours. So in these circumstances, some modication of the behaviour may be a good idea.

**Chasing squirrels**? Not a problem if you have vast tracts of land at your disposal in which to exercise your dog, but if you only have access to a small green encircled by roads, it might be wise to try and curb that dog's drive to chase.

**Licking faces**? Not a problem if you don't mind your dog licking your face. However, licking faces can lead to the asscociated practice of jumping up. So, if you don't want your dog to jump up at you, it might be a good idea to modify the behaviour of licking faces. If you don't mind your dog jumping up at you – well, again, there's no need to change anything. However, even if you don't mind your dog jumping up at you, there is a real risk that he will also jump up at other people. And that's not always welcome, especially if you've both been on a muddy walk and you happen across a child or a mother carrying a baby. And remember Mrs Robinson in her Sunday best coming out of church…

# WHEN IS A BEHAVIOUR A PROBLEM?

In conclusion, some behaviours aren't really problems as such. So cut yourself and your dog some slack. Sometimes, dogs are just being dogs. All we need to do is manage their behaviour and help the dog get over a problem behaviour or help him understand the behaviour is not really appropriate. Sometimes, context may mean we need to do nothing at all. However, behaviours can be a problem if:

1. The behaviour is causing your dog or another dog distress or harm.
2. The behaviour is causing you or other people distress or harm.
3. The behaviour or response is disproportionate to the stimulus.

In Chapters 11 and 12 we will look in detail at various problem behaviours that fall into at least one, and often all, of the above categories. But before we do, let's spend the next two chapters exploring and understanding how dogs' minds work. What makes them tick? Why do they do what they do? What are the major causes of behavioural problems? If we know this, we can avoid problem behaviours being established in the first instance. After all, life is so much easier for everyone if we can avoid the problem rather than trying to resolve it 'A stitch in time saves nine' and all that jazz…

# CHAPTER 2 –
# WHAT MAKES YOUR DOG TICK?

There are a number of factors that make your dog behave the way he does. It is important to bear in mind that he is simply trying to live life the only way he knows, and often, his behaviour is based on what he has learned works. It is never a case of him being naughty, bad or deliberately not listening and trying to dominate you. So, what drives a dog to do what he does?

## DOGS ARE NOT HUMANS!

Don't shoot the messenger, but… dogs are not humans. Dogs share 99.8% of their genetic makeup with wolves. I'm afraid that will remain the case, certainly in our lifetimes anyway. No matter how much we treat them like our babies, no matter how much we love them, no matter what name we give them – whether it be Frank, Brian or Steve – no matter whether our dogs sleep with us or take pride of place on the sofa (often to the detriment of our partners), they are born as dogs, identify as dogs and their behaviours are instinct based. We sometimes forget this and apply human logic and assumptions to our dogs' actions. We're not being insensitive, dim-witted or trying to undermine the authority of nature when we anthropomorphise dogs. We're just doing our best to understand the dog's world and so help our dog. This, however, can lead to misunderstandings and problems.

Take, for example, your dog being very happy to go outside on a dry sunny day but not liking going out in the rain. If you anthropomorphise his behaviour, you might think: "He doesn't like going out in the rain and therefore he must not like getting wet – just like us!" So, it makes sense for us to conclude that if we put a coat on him, he won't mind the rain so much – just like us! However, the dog's thought process is likely to be very different indeed. Rain amplifies noise, especially when it hits something like a conservatory's glass roof. Rain brings with it barometric pressure changes your dog can sense and is often accompanied by thunder and lightning; in the words of Queen's "Bohemian Rhapsody" – very very frightening! Moreover, ask yourself, does the amplified noise make it easier or more difficult for ears and noses to pinpoint prey? Undoubtedly the latter! And so, for a dog, not being keen on going out in the rain probably has little to do with him getting wet. Were that the issue, we probably wouldn't see many dogs rolling around in muddy puddles or having a swim.

Here's another example. You come downstairs and your little Barney has chewed the carpet. When you see this, you're a tad cross. Barney cowers, tail tucked under him, looks at you sideways and slinks away. If we anthropomorphise his behaviour, it seems that he knows that his actions are wrong and is now feeling guilty about the whole sorry affair! But research suggests that it's not guilt that is on display here. Barney's thought process is again quite different from our interpretation. In reality, since the incident probably happened a while before you arrived, Barney doesn't connect your reaction to his chewing. What Barney is responding to is you coming downstairs and – instead of reconnecting with him in the usual way, whatever that may be – acting in a rather threatening manner, with a stern look, pointing to the carpet in an inquisitorial manner and probably speaking in a loud voice. Barney is frightened, stressed and anxious about what you might do. You are now a 'situation' Barney wants to escape. He does this through submissive body language, desperately trying to appease and calm you.

## DOGS WANT TO BE PART OF YOUR SOCIAL CIRCLE

Dogs don't want to dominate you, they're not trying to be stubborn, and they're certainly not deliberately trying to make your life difficult. On the contrary, dogs wouldn't have the special place they have in our hearts (and sofas and beds) today, if not for the fact that they have, for thousands of years, wanted to be near us and to work with rather than against us.

*Large garden, but Frank and Ragnar are likely to stay close.*

Here are the five main reasons dogs *actually* don't listen to us:

**1. Your dog doesn't understand what you require of him**. You might think you've explained it clearly enough, but have you? It is believed that people have around 16 billion neurons in the cortex (the thinking part of the brain). Dogs, on the other hand, have around 550 million – not many, in the scheme of things. If your dog's pulling on the lead, shouting at him or yanking his lead isn't going to be a clear enough signal for him to understand that you want him to walk calmly on a loose leash. (More on loose-leash walking later.) Have you really been clear enough for your dog to understand that you don't want him jumping up at you? If you think you have, how come he's still jumping up at you?

**2. The reward for not listening is far greater than the reward for listening to you**. This is particularly evident when a dog is playing with his mates and the weary pleas of his exhausted owners for him to return to them fall on deaf ears. Playing with his mates, reading the various pee-mails and texts on the ground with his nose and duly responding to or chasing a squirrel is too strong a pull against 'come here' and essentially, 'stop playing'. We don't stand a chance, unless many months have been spent teaching our dog that brilliant things happen each time he comes to us, whether that brilliant thing is a great game, great food (and I don't mean a dry titbit that you've broken in half to eke it out!) or just you. Then, and with a fair wind behind you, you've got a good chance your dog will come to you when called. More on perfecting recall later.

**3. Age-related reasons**. Maybe your dog is just too young to understand how to do the things you want him to do. Or perhaps he's old and, due to physical aches and pains, finds it hard to come to you when called. Or, like many older dogs, he's suffering from canine cognitive dysfunction – similar to Alzheimer's in humans – which results in reduced responsiveness, disorientation and memory loss. Such symptoms can be confused with a dog not listening.

**4. You've taught him to ignore you**. Do you sometimes call your dog to you and when he doesn't come, you go to him and treat him anyway? Do you ask your dog to sit and when he doesn't, you ignore it and start doing something else? Do you pet your dog at his insistence? Do things generally get done at your dog's behest rather than yours? Did you forget to teach your dog basic manners such as the fact that an open door is not an invitation for him to barge through? Does your dog give those sad puppy eyes whenever you're eating and you, with your will of aluminium, end up giving him a morsel from your plate… and now it's got to the stage where he's virtually a few inches away from you, drooling like one of Pavlov's dogs? Guess what – you need to teach him not to ignore you and, through kind guidance, help him understand that good things only happen when he listens to you.

**5. Your dog doesn't trust you**. One of the major factors giving rise to aggression (lunging, barking, snarling, snapping, biting and all the attendant body language) is when a dog doesn't trust someone or something and worries that it might cause him harm. The use of physical force in training rather than kind and gentle guidance will contribute to this. Showing disapproval and annoyance and being impatient are off the table. I've often seen owners call their dogs, and when they're ignored, they shout at the dog aggressively. When the dog has eventually returned, or alternatively, when the owner has cornered him and grabbed his collar, the poor dog has then been reprimanded and shouted at again for having failed to listen in the first instance. There is a high probability that the dog will not listen to the owner the next time this happens.

*Does she trust you? Will she come running to you?*

Instead, what your dog needs is patience, a calming voice and touch, clarity of message, taking small steps and making learning fun. There's no better way of creating a strong bond than making your dog feel safe in your presence. Once he understands that you are there to look after his needs and deal with his anxieties and fears, you'll soon have him eating out of your palm.

# INHERITED / GENETIC BEHAVIOURS

Being visual animals, humans focus hugely on what specific breeds should look like when choosing a dog. When you buy a Rhodesian ridgeback, you may not want a dog that is 17 inches at the withers with a curly tail and short legs. And if you live in a small flat and want to buy a very small dog, it might be a little inconvenient if your puppy grows to be the size of a small horse! Breeders, for better or worse, have gone to a huge amount of effort to ensure specific breeds comply with physical breed standards. However, what owners rarely realise is that there is another standard that breeders have been developing: behavioural standards. Over the years, breeders have hypertrophied certain drives and behaviours for different breeds. So, if your dog is behaving in a particular way and your friend's dog isn't, you know why! These drives and behaviours become part of the inherited behaviours for that breed. So, Leonbergers love to swim, border collies love to herd, terriers love to dig, greyhounds love to chase, Dobermans prefer to guard, and spaniels love to chase birds.

This is where specific predatory motor patterns come in. These are explained more in a book by Raymond and Lorna Coppinger, *Dogs: A Startling New Understanding of Canine Origin, Behaviour, and Evolution*. Coppinger explains the basic motor pattern of a dog:

*EYE>STALK>CHASE>GRAB-BITE>
KILL-BITE>DISSECT>CONSUME*

Different breeds have had different elements of this motor pattern hypertrophied by breeders. For example, eye, stalk and chase have been exaggerated in a collie. Collies showing the subsequent motor patterns to grab-bite, kill-bite, etc. have been unselected for breeding. Collies with a tendency to grab and kill would clearly be a bit of a hindrance for farmers, and such behaviours are liable to get the poor collie 'reassigned' to less challenging duties – most likely followed by a lawsuit against the breeder who presumably promised a wonderful sheep-herding dog of immaculate parentage!

Terriers? No thank you to 'eyeing' the prey. No thank you to stalking. And no to grab-biting, dissecting and consuming, thank you very much. What a waste of time that would be for the owner of a working terrier used for eliminating rats. CHASE, KILL-BITE and then move on to the next rat, please.

So, if your dog is digging the heck out of your garden, herding your children or becoming protective as soon as a stranger gets too close to you, genes may be at play. When a dog is carrying out specific aspects of its breed's motor pattern, it is reinforced internally by the release of dopamine – something far more powerful than a titbit trying to persuade him to desist from, for example, chasing that squirrel.

Whilst some behaviours have been deliberately exaggerated within certain breeds, others creep in unintentionally. The temperament (the natural predisposition to react in a certain way to a stimulus[5]) of the sire and dame are often passed onto the puppies.[6] This means that dogs within the same breed have different thresholds – how easy or hard it is to elicit a reaction from them with regards to a wide

5      Burch, M. and Ljungren, D. (2019) 'Overview of the AKC Temperament.' Available from https://www.akc.org/wp-content/uploads/2020/01/ATT-OVERVIEW-FINAL-Aug-28-2019.pdf [Accessed on 10th November 2022]

6      Takeuchi, Y. and Houpt, K. A. (2003) 'Behaviour genetics.' *Veterinary Clinics: Small Animal Practice*, vol. 33(2):345–363. https://doi.org/10.1016/S0195-5616(02)00116-X

variety of stimuli. Just like humans, some dogs have low thresholds, some have high thresholds. Those with low thresholds are often introverted characters, whilst those with high thresholds are often extroverted. Generally, introverts tend to be weakened by social contact – it makes them withdraw into their shell even further. On the other hand, extroverts are strengthened by social contact. So, for a lot of dogs that are anxious and nervous, it is often because they have a low threshold to social pressure or stress. They get easily concerned by seeing new people or things in the environment. This concern can often manifest itself in 'aggressive' behaviours, including barking, growling, lunging and so on.

# REWARDS / REINFORCEMENT

Whenever a dog does a particular thing, there's likely to have been some environmental or other factor that influenced his behaviour and made him judge it to be the best course of action to meet his needs at that moment. But that behaviour is only likely to be repeated in similar circumstances if the dog is rewarded/reinforced AFTER he carries out the behaviour. In short, rewards maintain behaviour. For example, if the dog barks at the postman and the postman goes away (because he was always going to go away), the dog continues the barking because he was rewarded by the postman going away, which is what the dog wanted to happen.

So, dogs are likely to repeat behaviours for which they are rewarded and, conversely, unlikely to repeat behaviours for which there is no reward. This is operant conditioning, sometimes referred to as Skinnerism after its founder, Burrhus Frederic Skinner (1904–1990). Skinner's research showed that behaviours that are reinforced/rewarded tend to be repeated and strengthened, and behaviours that are not reinforced or are met with undesirable outcomes (punishments) are less likely to be repeated. Skinner's work did not address other factors such as emotions and chemicals that fuel or are present during the display of particular behaviours. He focused entirely on external and observable causes of behaviour, namely, rewards.

For reasons explained later in this book, I do not subscribe to the 'applying "undesirable outcomes"' part of Skinner's equation to stop unwanted behaviours. Briefly, this is because inflicting punishments on a sentient being is unnecessary; positive reinforcement is more humane and sufficient to get the behaviours you want. Furthermore, administering 'undesirable outcomes' can cause more problems than they may solve.

The important question is: what is a reward/reinforcement in the eyes of the dog? And again, we need to be careful not to attribute human qualities to dogs. Remember, anthropomorphism can cause misunderstandings and lead to problems.

## WHAT DOES YOUR DOG FIND REWARDING?

To some extent, the answer depends on what your dog is trying to achieve by any displayed behaviour. Remember, it's not just food, petting, kind words and games that your dog finds rewarding!

If your dog is jumping up at you when you come home from work, the motivation for the behaviour is most likely to be social bonding and/or a reunion after a period of isolation. The purpose (sometimes called 'function') of the jumping up is normally to gain your attention, social interaction and physical contact. In these circumstances, your dog is likely to find any sort of attention that you might give rewarding. In the dog's mind, you telling him to get off or yelling 'no' is a reward because he's got your attention. You pushing him off is a reward, because he's got the touch that he was craving. You looking at him is a reward because, again, he's gained the social interaction that he was seeking.

If your dog is barking at the postman, the motivation is likely that he wants to feel safe or alert you to a change in the environment, and the purpose of the behaviour is probably to drive the postman from the front door and to reduce the stress that the dog is feeling. In these circumstances, the postman going away (which he was always going to do) is a reward for your dog. When the dog manages to control the environment in this way, we call these sorts of rewards exogenous rewards/reinforcement.

But there is another category of reward/reinforcement that maintains behaviours. These are known as endogenous or internal rewards and consist of releases of chemicals in the dog's brain that have a positive effect on his mood. When your dog jumps at you, and you pet him, there are releases of endogenous opioids that make him feel good. Furthermore, looking at him and physical contact release oxytocin, not only in your dog, but also in you! If you're a mother, you're likely to have heard of oxytocin as the love/bonding hormone, copious amounts of which are released soon after you hold your baby after birth.

In conclusion, there are a number of reasons why dogs do what they do. And we know that exogenous and endogenous reinforcement make dogs repeat behaviours. Is there anything else that might impact them or cause them to behave in a particular way? What about emotions? Let's have a look at that in the next chapter.

# CHAPTER 3 – EMOTIONS

There is significant controversy about what emotions dogs feel and indeed whether they feel any emotion at all! Do dogs feel rage or anger like humans? Or is it the case that dog aggression is due to nothing more than the dog having learned that when he was aggressive in the past, he managed to get what he wanted? It is often said that whilst we can see the brain of a dog, we can't see the mind of a dog. We can't know what he's feeling, or indeed, not feeling.

I, however, fall into the camp that believes we *can* see the mind of a dog. We can do this by carefully observing his language. This is discussed further in Chapter 8. If you have a particular interest in this area and a general interest in neuroscience, I would recommend reading the work of Jaak Panksepp, particularly *The Archeology of Mind: Neuroevolutionary Origins of Human Emotions*, co-authored by Lucy Biven. In addition, I would recommend reading: Lisa Feldman Barrett's *How Emotions Are Made: The Secret Life of the Brain*. Much of the information set below on emotions is sourced from these two books and additional sources you can find in the bibliography.

There are basically two camps with differing views on emotions.

**The classical view** – In short, this view maintains that many behaviours are produced as a result of emotions. This view espouses the following:

1. Specific stimuli produce specific emotions. This means that emotions arise automatically in reaction to external stimuli in the environment. For example, if a dog sees a snake, the emotion circuitry of the fear system is likely to be activated.

2. Specific emotions produce specific responses/behaviours. In other words, each emotion produces a specific and distinct set of physiological and behavioural changes.

3. Specific emotions are produced in the oldest part of the brain (in evolutionary terms), sometimes referred to as the mammalian brain, which includes the limbic system, containing numerous structures including the amygdala, hippocampus, thalamus, hypothalamus, basal ganglia and cingulate gyrus.

4. There are seven different types of emotions that produce specific behaviours, and each emotion has a specific circuitry. There are four positive emotions (CARE, SEEKING, LUST, PLAY) and three negative emotions (FEAR, PANIC/GRIEF, RAGE).

Here are the six emotional systems that you are most likely to come across in connection with dog behaviours:

***PLAY*** – This emotional circuitry is positive and is characterised by pleasure and rough-and-tumble activities. The play system helps brain growth. As behaviourists, we like the play system because if it is activated, we know negative emotions and feelings such as anger, fear, pain and separation distress cannot exist at the the same time. Furthermore, the play system promotes growth factors such as Brain Derived Neurotrophic Factor, which promotes an anti-depressent effect. Play motivations are social (making and retaining social relationships and cooperation) and non-social (enhancing hunting abilities, physical skills and cognitive functions). Furthermore, when the play system is active, a specific mixture of chemicals are released, including endogenous opioids and cannabinoids, low doses of glutamate and some dopamine.

***SEEKING*** – This system relies on lots of dopamine release, which encourages intensive curiosity and investigative behaviours.

The seeking system promotes enthusiasm and motivation and is activated when an animal is seeking out basic survival needs such as food, sex, water or shelter, but when the dog is over-aroused it can lead to predatory behaviour. During activation of the seeking system, a dog is likely to display intensity in its behaviour: ears up, eyes and ears directed towards the stimulus, a tense body held expectantly, pointing posture, wide open eyes and forward body orientation. These behaviours are displayed at the start of the basic predatory motor pattern of Eye / Stalk / Chase / Grab-Bite / Grab-Kill. Too much intensity and arousal, and therefore dopamine, can very easily cause a dog to become agitated and impulsive and display over-reactive behaviours.

***FEAR*** – If the stimulus that could cause a fear response is far away, dogs are able to use the thinking part of their brain (the neocortex). But if the worrying stimulus gets too close, the limbic system (especially the amygdala, hypothalamus and periaqueductal gray) comes into play, which in turn activates the emotion of fear. This circuitry generates a negative mood which dogs find thoroughly unpleasant and from which they prefer to escape. Fear releases a cocktail of chemicals, including adrenaline, noradrenaline, cortisol, CRF (Corticotrophin releasing factor), ACHT (adrenocorticotrophic hormone), CCK, glutamate, alpha-MSH. It is the fear emotion that triggers the flight, fight, freeze responses, which you might be familiar with already.

*Body language asking for space.*

If the fight (aggression) response is triggered and the dog is successful in getting rid of the source of his fear, then, unfortunately, the response can generalise rather quickly to other situations and stimuli. Your dog being frightened of and barking at a Jack Russell across the road can quickly lead him to barking at every dog!

*RAGE* – This is another negative emotional circuitry. Rage is an emotion that mammals want to avoid, and it's closely linked to the neurochemistry of fear. If a dog can't escape something that is causing him fear, the rage system can become activated. Denial of access to resources, restraint and the ensuing frustration can also activate the rage system. Rage invariably results in aggression. Neuroscientists have discovered that major chemicals released during the rage system include substance P, testosterone, noradrenaline, adrenaline, and glutamate. We also know that neurotransmitters serotonin and GABA decrease rage.

*PANIC/GRIEF* – This system is activated when an animal feels distress caused by separation from someone close and on whom the animal is overly reliant. It's a survival mechanism. It starts early in young mammals, whose separation calls are designed to cause mum to seek them out and attend to their needs. When distressed by the absence of a loved one, glutamate and CRF chemicals are at elevated levels, and the stress response involving the release of stress hormones, including cortisol, is set into motion. This can cause a dog to panic and feel real, intense fear that can lead to him causing damage in order to reunite with his owner, potentially injuring himself. Dopamine releases in the brain predict that the owner will return and there will be a reunion. Once reunited, oxytocin and endogenous opioids are released to make the dog feel better.

Sometimes, dogs will display this behaviour when not truly anxious. Instead, if the dog is successful in getting the owner to return at the first slight whine or scratch at the door, it doesn't take long for the dog to work out and learn that barking, howling, whining, scratching at doors and creating a general hullaballoo soon results in the owner returning. This exogenous reinforcement also encourages dog vocalisations when the owner is parted from the dog.

*CARE* – This system is often activated and linked to resource guarding in un-spayed (and spayed) females when they have phantom pregnancies and they start to gather and guard toys. It arises from the seeking system so it's also fuelled by dopamine. Proximity to the desired resource releases oxytocin, prolactin, vasopressin and endogenous opioids. Without this care system and the protection afforded by the mother under its influence, it is unlikely that anyone of us would have made it into adulthood.

# THE ALTERNATIVE VIEW OF EMOTIONS – THE CONSTRUCTED VIEW

The main proponent of this view is Lisa Feldman Barrett. The constructed view challenges the classical view and maintains that emotions don't produce specific responses/behaviours. Instead, it proposes that variation in responses is the norm, and a dog's behaviours/responses are based entirely on how unpleasant or pleasant the stimuli are and on how aroused the dog is. On confronting a stimulus, the dog's brain makes predictions on what might happen, and the dog's response is based purely on past experiences as a guide.

Whichever view is right, or whichever view you subscribe to, the important thing to remember from a behavioural perspective is that:

a) Both camps accept that dogs feel pain, pleasure and distress. With that in mind, it is essential that we always treat our friends humanely and with respect and care.

b) Either way, the way dogs learn behaviours is still the same (more on that later).

c) Key neurotransmitters and hormones are involved, whether a dog is having an emotion (as suggested by the classical view) or behaving in a particular way based on how pleasant or unpleasant the stimulus is and based on previous experiences (as suggested by the constructed view). These include serotonin, dopamine, gamma

aminobutryc acid (GABA), glutamate, adrenaline, noradrenaline…
and a few others!

d) Whether the emotional part of the brain is activated (limbic
system) or the dog is highly aroused, the thinking part of the brain
is compromised. High limbic activation/high arousal levels = low
cortical activation! There's definitely a relationship between high
arousal levels and performance. Once arousal gets to a certain level,
performance dips. Ever seen a two-year-old child having a tantrum in
the supermarket? You can't reason with them at that stage! Similarly,
a puppy that has become over-tired or over-aroused is difficult to
reason with. This is the Yerkes-Dodson law of arousal, which we'll
discuss again in Chapter 6.

From a behavioural viewpoint, we're particularly interested in
the cerebrum. This comprises the **cerebral cortex** – the thinking part
of the brain that helps dogs learn new behaviours. The contrasting
part of the cerebrum is the emotional centre called the **limbic system** – the emotional part of the brain, which doesn't always bother
thinking, and influences both the nervous and the endocrine systems.

But, why are you telling us all this, Aftab, I hear you yell? Well,
there are three main reasons:

a) One set of emotions or feelings can flow into and become
something far more dangerous. For example, under the classical
view of emotions, PLAY can turn into SEEKING for one dog, and
FEAR for another dog. Under the constructed view, the pleasure
of PLAY and high arousal levels that come with it can turn into
unpleasant feelings and high levels of arousal that prevent the dog
from controlling his impulses. This can lead to predatory behaviours,
which can cause huge problems when a larger dog's PLAY turns
into SEEKING and a smaller dog's PLAY turns to FEAR. This, in
turn, can lead to the bigger dog biting the smaller dog as predatory
motor patterns become activated, with the bigger dog stopping only
when the smaller dog becomes limp. Another example of one set
of emotions or feelings turning into another would be a situation
where two dogs are in the middle of an altercation and the owner
reaches in to stop the disagreement by trying to pull the dogs apart.
This often results in the owner getting bitten. Why? Well, the dog
becomes frustrated by being restrained by the owner as he can't
get to the other dog. This frustration in turn can activate the RAGE
system. We know that when in a state of RAGE, a dog can become

even more aggressive. And if you're the one trying to restrain him, you're the one that is likely getting bitten.

b) Veterinarian involvement is hugely useful in assessing and, where appropriate, prescribing medication to counter various states such as general anxiety, fears, phobias and separation anxiety. Of course, medication alone is not the answer to these problems and is never, in isolation, going to resolve any behavioural problem. However, accompanied by a healthy dish of behaviour modification strategies, medications certainly can be useful in supporting behaviour strategies to modify the underlying causes that lead to undesirable behaviours/responses into something much more agreeable. Veterinarians are also useful in assessing and addressing any chemical imbalances or other underlying medical conditions that might exist and be contributing to the problem behaviours.

c) It's crucial to be aware of the hormones and neurotransmitters that cause, activate or help maintain certain negative emotions or feelings and those that are involved in certain positive emotions or feelings. Armed with this knowledge, you will be able to introduce activities for the dog that produce positive emotions and feelings, which, in turn, will increase chemicals that calm the dog and put him in a good mood and reduce stress. So, we know that the play system or engaging the lower levels of the seeking system are positive, beneficial and put the dog in a good mood. Since two separate feelings or emotions can't run concurrently, if the dog is feeling down in the dumps or anxious, we would definitely be aiming to lift his mood by introducing activities that engage, activate or promote his play or seeking system.

In short, in any given situation, the levels of chemicals will vary. To maintain homeostasis, the right amount of chemicals needs to be present at the right time. Too much or too little of any chemical at the crucial moment when a dog is exposed to any stimuli can produce unwanted behaviours.

Before we leave this subject of chemicals that fuel – or are at least present during – certain behaviours, it's worth mentioning some of the important chemicals involved and when they might be active. These include neurotransmitters and hormones. Neurotransmitters transmit signals directly across neurons in the brain and across nerve endings. They make us and dogs react in milliseconds! Hormones are released by secretory cells in various glands and enter the bloodstream. Hormones function outside the nervous system and their effects can be felt over hours, days, months and years. Puberty is all about hormones and is rarely an overnight thing.

**Serotonin** (a neurotransmitter). This is inhibitory in its effect and modulates the intensity of all emotions. It puts dogs into a good mood – elevated serotonin levels inhibit emotions, including fear. Reduced levels arouse emotions, including fear, and facilitate the dog becoming manic, hyper-emotional and impulsive. In this state, listening to you and general learning is mighty difficult. It's important that the amount released by the synapses is just the right amount at the right time, maintaining an equilibrium for that dog.

However, the above reflects current thinking. Science, as we know, is constantly changing. During my childhood, scientists believed that fat in your diet was bad. Now they tell us fat in your diet can be good. Indeed, there is already some evidence that some serotonin receptors might promote negative feelings.

**Dopamine** (a neurotransmitter). This is inhibitory in its effect and is associated with pleasure, motivation and reward systems. We've already learned that it is very much involved in the seeking system. If levels are too high, the dog becomes over-aroused, agitated, impulsive and over-reactive. Too much dopamine can also lead to repetitive behaviours. If the dopamine levels are too low, it can lead to the dog becoming underactive.

**Adrenaline** (epinephrine) and **noradrenaline** (norepinephrine). These are both neurotransmitters and hormones. Adrenaline affects heart rate, lungs and heart contractility, whilst noradrenaline causes the blood vessels to narrow and causes increases in blood pressure. These hormones activate the sympathetic branch of the autonomic nervous system and ready the body for the fight or flight response. Raised levels of adrenaline and noradrenaline are present when there is fear or rage or anxiety. However, whilst there is a correlation, that does not mean they cause these emotions. We do, however, know that reducing the levels of adrenaline and noradrenaline with medication has been found useful in calming, for example, anxiety.

**Gamma-aminobutyric acid (GABA)** (a neurotransmitter). GABA plays the role of inhibiting the effect of other neurotransmitters.

For instance, if certain behaviours are likely to arise in the event of too much dopamine having been released, GABA will inhibit the messages passing to other neurons to modulate the behaviours that may have otherwise arisen. Certain medications are used to enhance the effect of GABA. It is useful to know that GABA, although a key player in modulating, for example, anxiety, is not the only neuro-transmitter involved in doing so.[7]

**Glutamate** (a neurotransmitter). This is an excitatory neurotransmitter. Its presence can activate fears.

**Acetylcholine** (a neurotransmitter). This is also an excitatory neurotransmitter. Too much of this is likely to lead to behaviours such as aggression, anger and hypersexuality.

**Oxytocin**. Known as the 'love hormone', it not only helps form bonds between humans, but it has the same effect between dogs and humans. Physical touch or even looking at your dog releases oxytocin in the dog and you, and it makes us feel better! That's probably linked to the fact that oxytocin lowers the heart rate, blood pressure and reduces stress. No wonder people say owning an animal makes you live longer. Well, there have been occasions when Frank's behaviour has had the opposite effect, but in the long term…

Understandably, oxytocin is inhibitory in its impact on aggression. Oxytocin makes you a lover, not a fighter amongst your own social circle. The relationship between levels of oxytocin and a chemical called vasopressin is also relevant. Research shows that assistance dogs (specifically bred to have non-aggressive temperaments) have a higher oxytocin-to-vasopressin ratio than aggressive-type dogs.

---

7     Nuss, P. (2015) 'Anxiety disorders and GABA neurotransmission: a disturbance of modulation.' *Neuropsychiatric Disease and Treatment*, vol. 11: 165–175. doi: 10.2147/NDT.S58841

*Who's enjoying this cuddle more? Frank or Natasha?*

# CHAPTER 4 –
# MAJOR CAUSES OF
# BEHAVIOURAL PROBLEMS

There are many factors that that can cause, or at least contribute to, the development of troublesome behaviours that become ingrained in the dog's psyche. Let's consider some of the major causes of problem behaviours. Bear in mind that this is by no means an exhaustive list:

**a) Lack of socialisation with people, dogs and other animals**. You should positively expose your puppy to people, dogs and other animals in a variety of situations during his early formative months, and the experiences must be positive ones. The optimal window (the sensitive period) for socialising a puppy with people is remarkably short, from 3 to 12 weeks.[8] Some say the period lasts up to 16 weeks. This is the period when a puppy is developing resilience and flexibility, and you should use it to introduce him to all types of people: tall and short, barbigerous and bald, noisy and timid, green, black, blue, white, yellow, brown and any other kind of beautiful-coloured skin you might ever hope to find in the world. And not only that but people walking with a limp, wearing hats or sunglasses, groups of people, people in uniforms (including the dangerous and murderous postman and delivery drivers), children, babies and so on. The aim is to meet at least 100 people by the 13th week.

---

8      Howell, T. J., King, T. and Bennett, P. C. (2015) 'Puppy parties and beyond: the role of early age socialization practices on adult dog behaviour.' *Veterinary Medicine: Research and Reports*, vol. 6: 143–153. Available from https://www.ncbi.nlm.nih.gov/pmc/articles/PMC6067676/ [Accessed on 11th May 2020]

And whilst the optimal period for socialisation might be the first 12 weeks, it doesn't mean the socialisation window closes at 12 weeks or that after 12 weeks you don't need to bother anymore. It just means that if you have exposed your dog to positive experiences during that first 12 weeks, he'll be more readily able to deal with anything that he hasn't previously been exposed to, and is likely to cope more easily with a frightening experience.

This is the basic difference between a sensitive period and a critical period. A sensitive period is the time in which it is easiest for a dog to acquire a particular ability. A critical period, on the other hand, refers to a time frame after which a dog is unable to acquire a particular ability.

Socialisation efforts must continue through the dog's adolescent phase and right up to his social maturity. For bigger dogs, that can be up to around two and a half years! And even then you must not stop exposing him to positive experiences. To be frank, you should continue socialising your dog on a regular basis, forever!

And the same applies to socialisation with dogs. Big, little, hairy, not so hairy, old and young. All sorts of dogs. But again the experiences must be good ones. Quality rather than quantity should be your aim. You don't want to expose your puppy to a rude and unsocialised dog that is going to snap at or otherwise bully your young, impressionable puppy. When carefully socialised, as the puppy matures, he is less likely to display behavioural problems, particularly aggression, fearfulness and anxiety when confronted by other dogs.

I'm often asked how such extensive socialisation with other dogs is achievable prior to 12 weeks when the second puppy inoculation is often not until 12 weeks. Two points to remember here. First, lack of inoculation simply means that it may not be safe to put your pup on ground from which he may pick up some illness. It doesn't stop you from inviting people and dogs to your home. Socialising with people is much easier. Take your pup out in a rucksack, pushchair or in your arms. Whatever works. Maybe try driving somewhere and standing around with the pup in your arms, such as outside a supermarket. Believe me, you will have absolutely no shortage of admirers queuing to say hello to you and your puppy. But take it easy. We don't want to overwhelm him. Safe in your arms and at a distance that won't frighten him, your puppy can observe all types of animals. Make it your mission to stand by with the puppy safely off the ground and watch swans, ducks, cows, horses, sheep, etc.

Secondly, consider the risks of your puppy potentially catching something from socialising with other dogs against the risks of not socialising in this crucial sensitive period. Sure, don't take your puppy on an organised dog meet with 50 other dogs, or if you live in the USA, a dog park. But remember, your puppy will already have had his first inoculation before you pick him up at around eight weeks.

It is worth mentioning here that as a result of interaction with his mother and siblings between 5/6 weeks and 8/9 weeks, a puppy receives significant learning on what is appropriate/inappropriate interaction. Consequently, it is inadvisable to collect your puppy earlier than eight weeks.

*Ragnar the Ridgeback – at one with Daisy the chicken and Pippa and Pop the miniature ponies. Good early socialisation is crucial to animals living together in peace and safe meetings on walks.*

**b) Lack of habituation**. This is the puppy's gradual introduction to the general environment and all the inanimate things within it. Habituation is about helping the puppy understand that things in the environment don't signal anything important, that they just exist and are to be ignored, just like a sofa, a tree or a window. The optimal period is around 3–12 weeks. So, introduce him to the hoover, the lawnmower, tractors, cars, bikes, trains, buses, lifts, escalators, etc.

As always, the introduction should be gradual and at a distance or volume that doesn't frighten him. And remember, you shouldn't just expose your young pup to one car. Don't forget about the environment – a road on which he will see many cars.

A reputable breeder will have started the process of socialisation and habituation in the first eight weeks, prior to you collecting your best friend.

And what sort of problems might you encounter if your dog isn't socialised properly? The list is extensive: nervousness, aggression, fear, phobias and shyness for a start! Significantly, once these traits set in, it can potentially be a long and costly road to counterconditioning your dog's emotions and helping him live a happy and harmonious life with you.

**c) Traumatic experiences**. I've mentioned several times that you must always strive to ensure that the experiences to which your puppy or dog is exposed are positive. Three things to remember here:

First, dogs go through extremely sensitive periods where fears set in much more readily than at other times. It is important to note that between 8 weeks and 18 months, dogs go through an average of four fear periods. The periods are approximately:[9]

Between 8–10 weeks

Between 4–6 months

At about 9 months

Between 14–18 months

Secondly, when assessing whether an experience is positive or negative, try to see it from the puppy's perspective. Remember, something which might be so minor as to go unnoticed by you might actually be a terrifying experience for the puppy. For example, you might drop a pan on the hard tiled floor, causing a crashing noise. This is unlikely to have a lasting impact on you, as you'll just casually pick it up and resume your culinary endeavours. But for the puppy, whose hearing is four times greater than yours, it may have been both uncomfortable and absolutely terrifying. Or you might be walking past a bus when there's a hiss from the air brakes. Again,

---

9        *Regina Humane Society*. Available from https://reginahumanesociety. ca/programs-services/municipal-services/alternatives-to-admission/dog-behaviour-tips/puppy-developmental-stages-and-behaviour/ [Accessed on 10th May 2023]

you may take it in your stride, but it won't necessarily be so for the puppy. Similarly, a puff of smoke from a back-firing car might totally miss your attention, but for the puppy, being subjected to the shock of the exhaust pipe at his head level may ingrain it as a painful experience into his memory cells. As a result, he may come to regard all cars as extremely frightening and to be avoided.

This is classical conditioning at work. In a study, a boy was conditioned to be afraid of a white rat when previously he had been neutral about it. In a somewhat unethical experiment (clearly they thought otherwise in 1920), each time the rat (a neutral stimulus) was presented to the 11-month-old child, a hammer was used to make a loud noise just behind the child. This loud noise produced a startle response, an unconditioned response which 'involves reflexes, biology or bodily conditions'[10]. From thereon in, the wee child was afraid of rats! Through understanding classical conditioning, one can see how a dog might become afraid of children. For example, if a dog is resting and a child (neutral) accidentally stands on the dog's tail (ouch!), then in contrast to his previous neutral position, following the incident, whenever the dog sees any child, he fears that he will be hurt and seeks to escape the child through cowering or becoming aggressive to warn the child off. Frightening or painful events like these can result in intense permanent reactions to the same or similar triggers, can be difficult to overcome and can take time to eradicate.

Thirdly, how easily your puppy is scarred by any particular single-event learning experience does to some extent depend on his threshold levels (how easy it is to get a reaction from the dog to any given stimulus in the environment or social pressure). So, if you have a puppy with a low threshold to stimuli, you're going to have to be extra careful because the slightest change in the environment might be of major concern for the puppy.

**d) Medical conditions**. There is a whole host of 'medical' conditions that can contribute to a dog acting in a different manner from if he were feeling 100%. Behaviour changes can be a result of a physical ailment, such as an ear infection or arthritis or some other pain. We can all sympathise with that! The number of times I was far from welcoming to my children when they jumped on me or

---

10    Burch, M. R. and Bailey, J. S. (1999) *How Dogs Learn*. USA: Wiley Publishing, p.88.

wanted to play ball when my knee was playing up are too numerous to mention. The same really goes for dogs. Too many times I've seen dogs snap because they've been enthusiastically stroked when they are in pain. Similarly, an arthritic dog can snap when being forcibly moved off a sofa.

Moreover, the medical condition causing behaviour changes could be far more serious and involve a neurological disorder, such as epilepsy or a brain tumour. A number of symptoms/manifestations may indicate these conditions, including circling, head pressing and pain. Head pressing itself can be an indication of liver dysfunction, which can lead to a secondary brain issue. Perhaps behavioural changes such as irritability and aggression are caused by a medical condition involving the endocrine system, and are due to the production of an excessive or insufficient amount of hormones. This could result in Cushing's disease or hypothyroidism, hypoglycaemia or diabetes mellitus. Is your dog lethargic? Eating too much? Excessively urinating? Has your dog also recently become aggressive? If there's a suite of symptoms like these, a medical check-up is vital.

It is worth noting that medications themselves can cause behavioural changes. Steroids, for example, can cause an increase in avoidance behaviours, an increase in vigilant behaviour and a reduction in play behaviours.

**e) Us!** Owners often fail to appreciate the impact of their actions, and particularly the use of 'punishments', on their dogs' behaviour. As we have established, if your dog does something you like, you should reward him. And if he does something you don't like, you should ignore him, then wait a moment, and he'll soon offer a new behaviour to get your praise. That's the time to reward him again.

I'm often asked by clients what to do when their dog is doing something they can't ignore, such as chewing a table leg or saving your life (again) by barking his head off at the postman. Well, that's a great question. And it's true – ignoring him won't work if what he's doing is internally reinforcing his behaviour. This is where you have to distract him and offer him a more suitable alternative. Rather like if a child was drawing on the kitchen wall, we might, as an alternative, offer him a colouring book on which to direct and exhaust his artistic bent.

However, and too often, owners end up telling their dog off when he does something they don't want him to do. Now, there's a huge spectrum of what 'telling the dog off' involves. For example, imagine our dog is happily chewing on a table leg. Punishment-based responses might range from: shouting at him to stop it, shaking a can of stones, spraying water at him, moving towards him in an intimidating manner, dragging him away by the scruff of his neck, slapping his muzzle and kicking him. I'm very sad to say I've come across all these tactics being used by owners. I have also been shown video footage of a 'lady' sitting on the back of a bully-breed in an endeavour to make him submit when he had been boisterous. It made for a tear-jerking watch, as intermittently the dog submitted, and then tried to escape the weight of the 'lady' pinning him to the floor. Unfortunately, these types of tactics are fairly common in many parts of the world.

So, it's far better to gently redirect your dog away from doing something you don't want him to do by giving him the choice to do something else. When he does offer the behaviour you like, reward him immediately. This way, your dog is far more likely to repeat that behaviour you liked than if you punished him for the behaviour you didn't like. There are many problems with using force against dogs – and again, Dr Susan Friedman explains this really well:

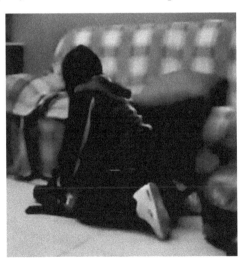

*Tear-jerking behaviour by a 'lady'.*

- It's unnecessary – if you simply reinforce behaviours you like and ignore behaviours you don't, those unwanted behaviours often just diminish. So, reinforce behaviours that are incompatible with or alternative to the unwanted behaviour. Don't like your dog jumping up? Just reward him whenever he doesn't jump up at you and has all four paws on the floor.

- It's also downright cruel – and you know it is. We know these behaviours displayed by dogs are normal. The behaviour meets the dog's needs at the time. You wouldn't punish your child for something that was normal, would you?

- It can also break or adversely affect the fantastically wonderful and rewarding bond you can potentially have with your dog.

- Often, it makes the dog temporarily submit. But there is no real behavioural change; the dog is likely to resort to displaying the unwanted behaviour when you aren't there. Moreover, if you tell a dog off for growling, snarling, barking, etc. – these behaviours are all intended as warning signals prior to a potential bite – next time, the dog might not display these warning signals but, if pushed, simply proceed to the final act of biting.

- It can cause apathy, avoidance behaviours and instil fear in the dog's mind. This then leads to various problems that are rooted in fear, including aggression. I am still amazed by the TV clip of Cesar Millan trying assert his dominance over a resource-guarding Labrador. When the Labrador says enough is enough and clamps on to Millan's hand, what does Millan do? Well, he certainly doesn't learn anything of value, that's for sure. No, he adopts a kung fu pose and tries to continue to assert his dominance over the Labrador. Even the Labrador must have been thinking "This bloke's either blind or stupid. I gave him plenty of signals to keep away."

- Punishment reduces learning. It's hard to learn when punishment increases stress and arousal to levels where the thinking part of the brain can't do its job – thinking! Ever tried to solve a problem when there's an almighty commotion going on? Punishment rarely teaches your dog the behaviour you actually do want instead of the behaviour you don't.

- Dogs often don't understand what they're being punished for. More often than not, the timing is all wrong and the dog simply doesn't make the connection between the behaviour and the ensuing punishment.

- As has been discussed, many behaviours are responses to a dog's emotions. In these circumstances, punishment is unlikely to change the mindset of the dog.

- Dogs often get accustomed to the severity or intensity of the punishment and so the punisher often has to raise the severity of the punishment for it to suppress the unwanted behaviour on the next occasion. And so it goes on, spiralling upwards until nothing less than kicking or choking the dog will suffice.

Two recent studies by Vieira de Castro et al. in 2020 make the case against aversive training methods.[11] One study of companion dog training found that dogs accustomed to punishment-based training methods displayed 'more stress behaviours during training, had higher elevations in cortisol levels after training and, if trained exclusively with aversive methods, were more "pessimistic" in a cognitive bias task than dogs trained with either reward and mixed methods.' The other study found that a secure attachment tended to be more consistent in dogs trained with reward methods.

There are many more unwanted side effects of punishment, but if you're not convinced with the above 11 reasons, I'm happy for you return this book to me for a full refund. This book is unlikely to be for you. That's because the rest of this book is all about teaching a dog to do things for you through positive reinforcement, rather than through intimidating tactics!

Whilst the above factors are, in my view, the main causes of behavioural problems, there are of course many other factors that can cause behavioural changes in dogs. For example, major upheavals in a dog's life, such as house moves, arguments in the home or new arrivals (see Chapter 10 on how to introduce new animals or a baby to the home). Dogs are also incredibly intelligent creatures and work things out pretty quickly! So, poor management of the environment and allowing a dog to practise unwanted behaviours can cause problems. You will be inundated with polite sits as soon as he understands the fact that whenever he sits you reward him. That bit is fine. However, you will equally see a repeat of your dog counter-surfing as soon as he realises that you leave food lying around on the kitchen worktops and that he is rewarded from time to time when he reaches up. Similarly, there might be much slipper chewing if you leave slippers lying around – a chew which is particularly

11 Vieira de Castro, A. C., Fuchs, D., Pastur, S., Munhoz-Morello, G., de Sousa, L. and Olsson, I. A. S. (2020) 'Does training method matter? Evidence for the negative impact of aversive-based methods on companion dog welfare'. *PLoS ONE*, 15(12): e0225023 10.1371/journal.pone.0225023

rewarding for your dog. So, start thinking about management of your environment several days before your new dog arrives!

# CHAPTER 5 –
# THE BULLETPROOF WONDER DOG

By now, you should have a good understanding of the causes of behavioural problems, and why your dog might behave the way that he does.

Your dog is likely to repeat behaviours for which he is rewarded. He is unlikely to repeat behaviours for which he is not rewarded or simply ignored, unless the unwanted behaviour is self-reinforcing, in which case you have to ask him to do something that you do like and reward him when he listens to you. Punishing your dog won't incentivise him to carry out behaviours you really want, certainly not in the long term, and furthermore, punishments can cause other problems.

Having established these principles, there is still a lot more to understand on the road to ensuring that behaviours that can lead to problems don't set in and that your dog matures into a confident and balanced dog that listens to you 100% of the time. Ok, the last aim is probably something that's only ever going to happen in your dreams and, to be perfectly honest, would be most abnormal. If that's what you crave, you're probably better off buying a robot dog.

So, here are some top tips to help your dog mature into the sort of dog that is confident in his skin, has agency to make his own choices, brings joy into your life and genuinely becomes a partner for you.

**Give him calm guidance and kind, gentle leadership.** Getting excited or frustrated when your dog is excited, boisterous or over-aroused simply adds to the excitement and pandemonium. Gently and clearly guide your dog to arrive at the behaviour you need. And this means that when your dog does do something that's not appropriate in the circumstances, there should be no annoyance on your part. Even the thought of using intimidation or punishment to enforce the behaviour you want should be ruled out.

**Be consistent.** Often dogs find it difficult to understand what is required of them because some members of the family will be reinforcing certain behaviours whilst others are singing from another hymn sheet altogether! Take, for example, my client Martin and his wife, Penny. Their issue was with their handsome labradoodle, Larry, constantly hovering around the dinner table and begging – a behaviour that could have been resolved within a matter of days. Well, it had been several weeks, and Larry still hadn't got the hang of it. This was despite the fact that I had demonstrated to the couple how to teach Larry to stay on his bed a few metres from the table, and told them to practise the strategy regularly and each time they were at the table.

Guess what? It turned out that whilst Penny had been quite strict with this, Martin, the softy in the family, had from time to time given Larry titbits from his plate and not insisted on Larry staying on his bed! To compound the problem, the children had been literally feeding Larry's begging habits regularly and certainly weren't, or were incapable of, insisting he stayed on his bed whilst they were at the table.

Sometimes, it is the lack of consistency from different members of the family that prevents a dog from learning as quickly as he might otherwise have done. Sometimes it's due to the *same* person using different cues. You want your dog to come to you when called? Well, it would seem common sense that always using the same word would be a start. However, I have come across clients that sometimes say 'come', sometimes 'here, boy' and sometimes 'come here!'. The latter is normally in a stern voice and used when the dog hasn't complied with the initial request. How is a young dog to learn a new human language when a different word is used for the same request?

In addition to consistency, remember insistency and persistency. If you're going to ask your dog to do something, make sure you have the time and inclination to help guide him to carry out the request. Don't ask for a sit and then when he doesn't, ignore it and carry on with your household chores, as this will end up poisoning the cue. Furthermore, your dog will begin to have little regard for anything you say and start to see you as just someone that makes a noise. But do persist with training. It can take time for dogs to learn a new 'language'. Humans have 16 billion neurons in the cortex, and it takes us a couple of years to master a few words and sentences. Dogs? Well, they've got around 500 million neurons and their communication is largely based on scent, sight and hearing. Dogs do not have a language processing area in the brain like humans, so you need to keep at it.

## MEET YOUR DOG'S ESSENTIAL NEEDS

In my opinion, Abraham Maslow's hierarchy of needs model of what is necessary for humans to achieve their full potential and therefore happiness equally applies to dogs. The five needs identified by Maslow are:

> *"1. Physiological needs – air, water, food, shelter, sleep, clothing, reproduction*
>
> *2. Safety needs – personal security, employment, resources, health, property*
>
> *3. Love and belonging – friendship, intimacy, family, sense of connection*
>
> *4. Esteem – respect, self-esteem, status, recognition, strength, freedom*
>
> *5. Self-actualisation – the desire to become the most that one can be."*[12]

Translated to dogs, this could be broken down into three essential needs as follows:

**Physiological needs –** This is all about good and appropriate nutrition, air, sleep, indoor shelter, safety, warmth, gentle grooming, veterinary care and fresh water, as well as sufficient exercise. Exercise helps produce serotonin, which is known for aiding relaxation as it dampens emotions and intense behaviours and the motivational urges in the brain. These physiological needs are the things that are essential in order to provide a dog with the heathiest foundation possible and are an absolute must to raising a balanced dog. Without them, behavioural problems will inevitably develop due to a range of disparate reasons. It's also an area in which most loving

---

12      McLeod, S. (2023) 'Maslow's Hierarchy of Needs.' *Simply Psychology.* Available from https://www.simplypsychology.org/maslow.html

and caring dog owners generally excel without much trouble. On the Maslow's hierarchy of needs, these equate to the basic needs, which encompass the psychological and safety needs.

**Emotional needs** – This is all about trust, calm and gentle leadership, consistency, love (that's an easy one for most dog owners), bonding and play with people, bonding and play with other dogs and a calm environment. It's also about the dog having access to a quiet place to sleep and rest without the chaos of family life, using positive methods of training – no force (yes, I've said this before several times and I will be repeating this until it's second nature to you), the dog feeling safe and having fun. From my experience, the majority of my clients are generally able to tick off 60–70% of these needs before I start working with them. For a truly happy and well-rounded dog, we need to be getting close to meeting 100% of these emotional needs.

*Playing with friends.*

**Enrichment needs** – This is all about having a rich and varied life. In order to enrich your dog's life, you need to provide opportunities in the environment to ensure enrichment in the six key areas set out below. Many of the activities in each area will overlap with activities in other key areas. What's more, some of these activities are passive – they don't involve much, if anything, on your part. Other suggested activities are somewhat more active – you are involved. Active activities provide a double bonus for you and your dog. Petting, looking at and playing with your dog releases oxytocin in both you and your dog. This helps forge strong bonds between you – crucial if you are going to have a truly wonderful and lasting friendship and if you want your dog to do things for you, rather than because of you. A true partnership.

**Cognitive enrichment or mental stimulation** – This means providing opportunities for your dog to use his brain. Rather than just putting his food in a bowl, make him think about how to access his food! Teach him new cues (sometimes still called commands), new tricks, names of toys, the difference between left and right and so on. What about hiding some food and asking him to find it?

**Social enrichment** – This involves providing opportunities for your dog to play with other stable, confident and well-socialised dogs. There are social and non-social benefits for your dog when he indulges in rough-and-tumble play with other dogs. Play with people is also part of social enrichment. What about playing hide and seek? What about using a flirt pole with a ball or a bunch of feathers on the end of the line? You could simultaneously use this as an opportunity to get your dog to use his brain – go all advanced mode, and at the same time really rein in his impulse control and teach him to leave, drop, and chase only when you request it.

**Environmental enrichment** – Make the living space interesting for your dog. New toys, a digging pit, a tunnel, a ball pit… anything, really, that your dog can investigate. Dogs are neophiles. So change things around rather than constantly leaving all his toy paraphernalia lying around.

**Feeding enrichment** – Some of the activities in this category often overlap with cognitive enrichment. Rather than a bowl of food, why not scatter the food all over the lawn and let your dog have a great time using his nose to find the food? Each time he finds a piece of kibble, he releases dopamine, a neurotransmitter crucial in learning. Put his food in a stimulating, slow-release food or treat dispenser such as a Kong toy. He'll love taking time in working out how to get at the food. This doubles up as an activity that enriches his brain. Eating from a Kong may take him 15 minutes or so rather than just wolfing it down in 30 seconds! How about hiding food under a blanket? Scattering some food into a ball pit? All this enables your dog to use his natural hunting and foraging skills, which is intrinsically rewarding for dogs.

**Sensory enrichment** – Imagine being at nursery as a child with white walls and not much else. Ever seen animals in poorly resourced zoos? They are bored and, as a result, problem behaviours often set in, including destructive behaviours and compulsive behaviours such as rocking and so on. So try to provide an environment that will stimulate your dog's senses, particularly smell, taste and touch. Anything to arouse his curiosity and provide a challenge. This will automatically overlap with and satisfy his cognitive enrichment needs.

*"Now how da heck I get to da treat?!"*

## Training

The importance of training your dog to understand at least some basic cues is clear to most people. However, I do sometimes get asked what the point of this training is, particularly when I'm lecturing abroad, where dogs often live outdoors and are treated less as family members than they are, say, in the UK or USA. So, let's deal with this question first. There are a number of reasons for teaching your dog some basic cues. It's great for mental stimulation, creates a bond between you and your dog and, of course, if you're going to live together, it's useful for you to understand 'doggy language' (more on this in Chapter 8) and for your dog to understand human language. Crucially, teaching certain cues is vital to ensuring your dog's safety. If he's picked up something dangerous, it's useful to have a way to make him drop it. If you haven't managed the situation well and he happens to get a tad too close to passing traffic on a nearby road, he really needs to understand how to stay or come back to you when asked. If you don't want him to potentially injure his neck and cause you a bad back because of him constantly pulling on the lead, you need to teach him how to walk on a loose leash.

So, which basic words might be useful for your dog to understand if you are to live together harmoniously? Whilst that is a personal decision for each owner based on their personal circumstances, I find teaching a dog the following **seven cues** is a good start: *Sit, lie down, bed, stay, come, drop it, and heel* (loose-leash walking). Anything else? Sure, why not. Research shows that the average dog can learn around 165 words. And the genius dogs amongst us? 1200 words for a particular collie named Rico! Maybe you have a prodigy in your midst. So, go for it! And whilst you're at it, teach him some basic arithmetic. Remember, dogs can count, too… certainly up to five.

But I would caution against a few particular words. The first is *NO*. It's a negative command, and so often a gateway to using intimidation and force-based training tactics – albeit at the lower end of the spectrum. Furthermore, the constant barrage of 'NO' can get a bit tiresome for you and the dog, especially during the puppy phase, when he is doing exactly what comes naturally to him and, quite appropriately, exploring everything in his environment. Better to manage your environment and ask your dog to carry out an alternative behaviour (e.g., 'sit') when he does something you don't like and can't ignore, coupled with lots of rewards when he offers you the suitable alternative behaviour.

For the same reasons, you don't even have to teach your dog to 'leave it' or 'off'. That's because these cues are requests for no behaviour rather than a different, mutually exclusive behaviour. But I know owners struggle with not teaching their dog to 'leave it' or 'off'. So, fine. It's not one of the 'crimes' for which you should be incarcerated. However, make sure you reward your dog when he does something you do like.

The other word? **Paw**. Yep, it's cute – especially if you have a small dog. But for a large breed? Cute when a puppy, not so cute when he's fully grown and paws you when you're least expecting it. Ouch. Especially where children or an aged family member is involved. Also, when you've just returned from a muddy walk? Again, not so great.

# CHAPTER 6 – GUIDANCE ON TRAINING

Whether you've just taken on a new puppy or an older dog – maybe it's a rescue – as we just established in Chapter 5, it's essential that you train him on some basic cues. Here are some of the most important tips I've learned over the years that will help you get the best out of your dog.

- Different dogs learn at different rates. So, take your time. It's not a race. Remember that the frontal cortex of a human brain doesn't really come 'online' until we're around 25 years of age, and your dog's will take time to develop as well. What is the purpose of this part of our brain? Postponing gratification, stopping our impulses from making decisions for us, planning a course of action, etc. Basically, it's used for thinking before acting. So, why expect your puppy to get everything right straight away? Don't be hard on yourself either.

- Persist in training. I heard a great analogy once. When you're out of shape and you go to the gym for an intense session, you are hardly likely to see immediate change in the mirror! Most people quit the gym because they don't see that change after just a few sessions. Thousands of people join the gym in the New Year and by February/March they've had enough. However, if you persist and commit to going regularly – sure, you have cheat days and miss the odd day, but if you persist – you will eventually get into shape and start to notice a difference. Training a dog is very similar. It's not about the event of going to the gym or doing a training session with your dog. Nor is it about the intensity of the session. It's consistently going to the gym and the dog training sessions that makes the difference.

So, persist. But also, try to enjoy the goofy and tricky months of training – which can last up to two and half years. You'll look back at them fondly – just as we look back with fondness at all the things our children took ages to understand. My children are now aged 30 and 32. Even so, whilst they've learned to switch lights on, they've still yet to master switching them off when leaving the room.

- Don't repeat commands. You really want your dog to sit on the command of 'sit', not on the command of 'sit, sit, sit'! Repeating cues simply poisons them. The dog begins to understand only that it doesn't matter whether he listens or not and ends up following instructions when he wants to.

- Train when you have time. Training never stops. In fact, training is constant – it has to be, because your dog is constantly learning. But certain things that are a bit more complicated need a bit more planning. Make sure you're not squeezing it in between telephone calls, or when you're just about to leave for work, or just as the kids are coming downstairs in urgent need of breakfast and running late for school!

- Keep training sessions short and set your dog up to succeed. Try not to engage in training exercises for longer than 15 minutes. Training is mentally demanding for both you and the dog, and the attention span of young dogs is quite short. For this reason, short, sharp, focused and regular sessions are far more preferable to one long session. If you overwork your dog or the task is too difficult, he is likely to become frustrated and over-aroused. If that happens, you won't get the best out of him. That's because there's a relationship between arousal and performance. As arousal increases, performance also increases. However, there is a point on the arousal scale beyond which performance dips. This is known as the Yerkes-Dodson law. Arousal or stress beyond a certain point adversely affects control and performance, and you then get a dog that starts to play up, biting and tugging on the lead and basically playing silly beggars. That, in turn, is likely to lead to you getting frustrated, shouting, generally getting annoyed and wondering what on earth is wrong with your dog.

- Make training fun and learn through play. This really is crucial for everyone's well-being. Montessori teaching for children worked this out a while ago, and now this teaching method is de rigueur throughout the early years system. Unsurprisingly, it's the same for dogs. If you get it right, your dog won't even know he's learning. For him, it will just be another game (great) with rewards to boot (double great!). When learning through play, there are releases of endogenous brain opioids. Social play with owners (even just looking into the dog's eyes) releases oxytocin and vasopressin, which enhance the opioid effect of good emotional feelings. In turn, this reduces stress and anxiety.

*Have fun – make it a partnership.*

- Use reward-based training methods only. Oops, there I go again. Reward, reward, reward. Praise, praise, praise. No shouting, no force, no intimidation, no punishments, no getting annoyed and no disapproving looks – trust me, they won't work. You'll end up weakening the bond of trust that you desperately need to build and maintain to get the best out of your dog.

FMRI scans can show when dogs are feeling pleasure. That's when they work best and are more likely to listen to you. Under test conditions, FMRI scans showed that for many dogs, the same amount of dopamine was released from praise alone as when they were given treats. And as we've already discussed, when you stroke your dog, oxytocin (a.k.a. the love hormone) is released for both him and you, helping form bonds.

- Repetition. Ever tried to learn something new? What works best – one long session learning lots of new things and then nothing for a while, or repeating one or two tasks only, several times a day? I know what works for me. Keep it simple. Help your dog understand and fully get to grips with one or two things during each session. Repetition means your dog learns better and remembers things for longer periods. As they say, practice makes perfect.

• Timing of rewards. Make sure your dog understands and makes the connection between his actions and the reward. For him to do that, you must reward him within two seconds (quicker if you can) of him doing whatever you asked of him or him offering you a behaviour that you want him to repeat. So often I see people call their dog, and what do they do when the dog happily goes to them? They ask him to sit. The dog obliges and he is then rewarded. As far as the dog is concerned, he's been rewarded for sitting, not the recall. Alternatively, the dog runs back as requested and the owner fumbles around in his pocket and several seconds later the dog is rewarded. The dog has no idea why he's been rewarded as he's lost the connection between the action of returning and the reward.

It is important to be aware of what trainers refer to as the 'Three Ds' in training: Distance, Distraction and Duration, all of which impact your dog's performance. Training is like charity: it begins at home, where you will find little distraction as the dog should be familiar with and habituated to the environment. Therefore, if you're training a sit or recall, start in the house. Then move to the back garden, where there will be a few more distractions, followed by the front garden and its noisier distractions. Next, maybe progress to the street, but without other people and dogs, then progressing to with another dog or person/people in the distance, and so on. You get the point. It's all about the level of distractions.

With distance, you may initially need to practise recall from a foot or two away. When asking your dog to sit, you might start next to him, then gradually increase the distance. However, when you increase the challenge in one area – for example, you increase distance – you'll need to decrease the challenge in another area – e.g., distraction.

When considering duration, it is futile and rather frustrating for you and your dog if you ask for a sit, stay or down for five minutes when you haven't built up the duration of the cue. So, start with a couple of seconds' duration. Small steps please. And remember, increasing the challenge in duration will involve reducing the level of challenge presented by distraction and distance. This way, you set your dog up to succeed – for which he quite rightly gets a reward. But so do you. So, give yourself a pat on the back too.

• With rescue dogs, you have to move very slowly, especially for the first few weeks and sometimes months. You might not get any of the problems around teething, toileting and so on that you get with puppies, but the majority of rescue dogs come with considerable emotional baggage that you, in due course, are going to have to confront and help them to overcome. It can take several weeks for a rescue just to show his true self. Despite the best of intentions, rescue centres can be very stressful places for dogs.

Focus on meeting the three essential needs of your rescue dog, namely physical needs, emotional needs and mental stimulation needs. It's crucial that you spend time getting to know him and understanding his level of knowledge. He may never have heard a washing machine or a vacuum cleaner before. Additionally, take your time in launching into a strict regime of training. Let him find his feet and when you have formed a bond, then start some training to help him understand the requirements of his forever home. Building up positive conditioned emotional responses to everything that troubles him should be your initial focus with rescue dogs.

- Rewards/reinforcement. Your dog will repeat behaviours that are reinforced for him. Reinforcement doesn't just come from food. It can also be done with games. Which one to use? Well, both really. Food rewards are very reinforcing but can decrease in value after the twentieth treat as the dog can become satiated by food. On the other hand, play that taps into a dog's predatory drive causes a release of dopamine, which never decreases in value for the dog, so the dog will not become satiated by the game. With young puppies, food treats are better as the training session ends well before the puppy gets satiated and the intensity of the reward for play is not as strong for a 5-month-old puppy as for a 12-month-old dog. Conversely, for older dogs, play is often better. Trainers of working dogs such as gun dogs often don't bother with food treats, as the dopamine released by the chase and retrieval of the shot bird is far more of an effective reinforcer than any piece of cheese or kibble.

In terms of how often to reward your dog: personally, I'm very happy to reward Frank every time he does anything for me – he's such a cutie pie. Often it's a food treat, but if I'm running short then the rewards are interspersed with a 'good boy' or a stroke under the chin.

Arguably, different reward ratios should be used for specific cues to get the best performance. So, let's just touch on this.

- o If you're trying to teach an episodic behaviour like 'come' or 'bark', then initially reward every time you get the requested behaviour. Once the behaviour is secure, then eventually, you should reward at a variable rate. This means mixing it up and rewarding on the third time, then the first time, then the fourth time and so on. I would try to never leave it longer than four correct behaviours before rewarding. Leaving it too long risks the dog thinking the behaviour is no longer desired.
- o If you're trying to teach a continuous behaviour like 'stay', then initially reward at fixed intervals and eventually move to variable intervals. This means rewarding after different periods of time. For example, on the first occasion rewarding after 20 seconds, and then on subsequent occasions after different intervals such as 40 seconds, 10 seconds, 60 seconds, and so on.
- Lure, Capture, Prompt, Shape and Proof: these are some of the strategies you are most likely to use when training your dog using force-free, reward-based methods.
  - o **Lure.** Guide your dog into the position you want using something he will follow. Typically, this will be a treat. You want your dog to sit? Hold a treat in front of his nose, and as he engages with the treat, lift the treat up and back, and your dog will sit. Pushing his hindquarters down to try to get him to sit is not really the way forward – you could hurt the dog, and it becomes a question of who's stronger, since the dog will naturally push back. What's worse is that you have now started using a technique the dog finds unpleasant. Luring is great when first training a dog. Remember that you should eventually 'fade' luring out as otherwise it turns into bribery and your dog will then only do things when there's a treat about! The lure needs to transition to a verbal or visual cue where the treat is presented after the fun activity has been performed.
  - o **Capture.** This is where a dog does something and you signal to him that you approve of what he's done and then reward him. Rather like taking a photograph of his action and showing him that the action was what

you wanted. Some people use a clicker to tell the dog. Alternatively, you can just say 'yes' or 'good'. By way of example, imagine your dog wants a stroke and he comes up to you and puts his head on your lap. You like that? Signal that you like that behaviour by saying 'good' or a click and then follow it up with a reward – within two seconds!

- o **Prompt.** This is about helping your dog make the right choice using physical assistance so minimal that it is not regarded as aversive. In other words, a prompt is a strategy used to increase the likelihood of a wanted behaviour so it can be rewarded. For example, if you were walking by the river with your two year old child and you didn't want the child to go into the river, you might hold his hand to prompt him not to get any closer to the river as you continue with your walk or watch the ducks. If you're training a recall, you might have your dog on a lead, preventing him running off somewhere else (no tugging or yanking the lead – that is aversive, and isn't really giving the dog the option to do the right thing). When he does return to you, reward, reward, reward! Another example of a prompt? If you're teaching your dog not to pull on the lead, you might use a hedge or wall and your leg to block him from going ahead of you to prevent him from pulling.

- o **Shape.** Essentially, if you reward approximations of the required behaviour, then those approximations eventually become the behaviour. For example, if you want to teach your dog to shut the door, initially, you might reward him for just touching the door with his nose. This can progress to rewarding him when he pushes the door a bit harder and the door moves and so on until he eventually closes the door.

- o **Proof it.** Dogs don't generalise training very well. Despite having taught your dog to sit in the front room, he may have trouble when you ask him to sit in the garden or on the pavement. And this is not just about distractions. Dogs are, to some extent, neurodivergent. A neurodivergent child may have difficulty understanding whether the smile of a stranger has the same meaning as the smile of his mother. Whilst smiles are universally similar, there are differences that may be picked up and misunderstood by a neurodivergent child. Similarly, dogs are not just responding to your cue of 'sit'. They're taking in the surroundings, precisely how you're standing, the distance between you and them, and so on. Here's an experiment for you to try. Teach your dog to sit in the kitchen area whilst standing directly in front of him with your hands clasped across your midriff (as if you were – and probably are – holding a treat). Next, ask him to do the same thing in the garden, whilst standing four feet away, with a tree behind you, on one leg, with your hands above your head. Did he sit? Probably not. So proof your training in a variety of places, times, clothes, weather conditions and generally diverse environments.

I worked with a lovely Cane Corso recently, called Snoopy. The owner had trained him well and proudly demonstrated this. The owner put the food bowl down, asked Snoopy to stand by his side, then go around him, then go through his legs, then shake with his left paw, then shake with his right paw, then come from behind and sit under the owner's legs and, finally, Snoopy was required to kiss the owner before being released to eat his food. Snoopy performed brilliantly. The owner had done well. But this was all in the kitchen. I asked the proud owner whether he could get a similar level of focus, attention and obedience in the garden. Of course the answer was no. That was predictable and a shame. I was actually there to deal with Snoopy's over-reactivity towards other dogs. If only the owner had had a similar level of attention from Snoopy in a more challenging environment with additional distractions. The owner could then have asked Snoopy to focus on him rather than focusing on other dogs and thus avoided the reactivity issue.

Always remember, there are four stages to learning:

1. Acquisition – This is about your dog beginning to understand what you need from him and when.

2. Fluency – This about your dog getting it right regularly.

3. Generalisation – This is about your dog being able to get the behaviour requested right in all sorts of situations, places and times, taking into account distance, distraction and duration.

4. Maintenance – The newfound skills of your dog need to be practised regularly so they become well-ingrained and not forgotten. Imagine if you became a proficient pianist and then didn't practise regularly…

# CHAPTER 7 –
# TRAINING BASIC CUES

There are two important things you should take away from this chapter. First, using reward-based methods rather than force will be better for you and your dog in the long term. Furthermore, the bond between you will grow and you'll get your dog wanting to do things for you and for praise, rather than out of concern because of you. As a result, you are more likely to have a dog that trusts you and is comfortable in your company. Using force is an unnecessary, morally unacceptable, lazy way of training and is, frankly, cruel.

Secondly, for many cues, introduce your chosen word for the cue after your dog has actually started to do whatever you're trying to teach him to do. Use the tools of luring, capturing, prompting and shaping (as discussed in Chapter 6) to show him what he needs to do.

Teaching your dog the seven cues of **sit, lie down, stay, bed, come, drop it and heel** (loose-leash walking), is always useful. This book is chiefly about problematic behaviours rather than training relatively straightforward cues like these and there is plenty of information on how to train these cues online; so for these reasons, I'll be brief. I'll focus only on a few of these cues and particularly on what not to do, along with some tips that you might not have seen mentioned by others:

- **Sit.** Most owners find this the easiest cue to teach their dog. As I've said previously, hold a treat between your finger and thumb, near the dog's nose. With your palm facing upwards, move the treat up and back over the dog's head and down a bit. Your dog should follow the treat with his nose and naturally come to a sit. Reward! This is luring in action. When he's getting this right all the time, THEN introduce the cue of 'sit', just as he sits. Repeat. If your puppy is having difficulty, having him stand in front of a wall might help so he doesn't keep shuffling backwards. It's also a useful behaviour to teach your dog as a behaviour that is incompatible with other behaviours, such as jumping up. But it's not essential. Indeed many dogs, such as hounds, because of their physiology, find it more difficult to sit than breeds such as poodles. Also, innately, dogs don't really sit much. They stand and they lie down. Nevertheless, the cue is extremely useful in a number of ways: strengthening inhibitory processes, impulse control, lowering arousal levels, preventing your dog from getting more excited, and as a gateway to getting him to focus on you.

If you do want to teach your dog to sit, here's what not to do. Don't use pressure on his hindquarters to push him down. He'll naturally push up, you'll get into a struggle of who's stronger, and you could end up damaging his joints. AND you're no longer using positive reinforcement methods for training. This type of method uses negative reinforcement, involving the introduction of something the dog finds unpleasant and only removing that unpleasantness once the dog has done what you wanted. This is unnecessary and can be counterproductive.

• **Down.** It may help to teach this from a sitting position, with a wall behind the dog. Whilst the dog is in a sitting position, hold the treat between your thumb and index finger and move the treat down and between his front paws. This time, have your palm facing towards the floor. This should help the dog to lie down. Be patient. This can sometimes take a while for young puppies. They never quite like to lie down and often start shuffling their bottom or nibbling at the treat whilst technically still sitting, albeit quite low down. In these circumstances, reward your dog when you get an approximation. This is shaping. Over time, you will get a complete lie down. Again, as a progression, once he's consistently completely lying down, introduce your cue of 'down'. After some practice, try going from 'down' to 'sit' and then 'sit' to 'down' BEFORE rewarding him with a treat. Incidentally, the reason for having your palm facing down as you place a treat between your puppy's legs is that you will ultimately want to ask him to lie down from a distance. Moving your hand with the palm down at this stage is the beginnings of a gesture you may want to use when asking him to lie down, by signalling the request with your hand moving in a downwards motion.

- **Stay.** If you teach your dog to lie down or sit, the cue of 'stay' is actually somewhat superfluous. He should stay sitting or in a down position until you release him. But I know a lot of people like this cue. Also, you may want him to simply stay in one place without wanting him to be in a sitting or down position. The word "hold" would be a better cue, as I have taught Frank and Ragnar. So, let's deal with this one. As with 'sit' and 'down', the thing to remember is to build up the length of time the dog stays in the correct position. Start with one second before slowly extending the time, but in a zigzag time pattern. One second, three seconds, two seconds, five seconds, one second, seven seconds, etc. Always end the exercise after the longest period of stay with a release cue. When practising this cue, remember to consider and experiment with distance, distraction and duration, as discussed in the last chapter.

- **Bed.** You'll also have to practise the 'Three Ds' when you're teaching your dog to chill out on his bed. Help your dog learn to go to and stay on his bed by throwing a treat on his bed. Occasionally, you can walk him on a lead to his bed and, as soon as he's there, drop a treat on the bed. Once he's on his bed, keep treating him. Initially, you might want to treat him even if he just puts a paw or two on his bed. This is 'shaping' the behaviour, as discussed in the last chapter. Eventually, only treat him when he's fully on his bed. And if he doesn't initially lie down, don't worry about it. Treat him anyway.

Eventually you'll want to treat him when he's lying down in bed – you can ask him to lie down, or just wait as he might just lie down of his own accord; in which case capture this (mark the good behaviour by clicking or saying 'yes' or 'good') and treat him.

When you're using treats to get him to his bed, do some fake throws. If he goes to his bed, treat after he's got there. These fake throws are the beginnings of hand signals asking him to his bed.

As always, introduce the cue of 'bed' when your dog is actually on his bed. Make sure you call him off his bed before he makes the decision to get off. Extend the time on his bed slowly and in a zig-zag timeline as discussed under 'stay' above. Ultimately, you want to leave him there and go about your own business for increasing lengths of time before treating him or calling him off the bed and duly rewarding him.

For longer stays, give him something to chew on his bed. My dog's preferred chew? Try a moonbone. Yum. And it lasts for ages! Also, unlike a pig's ear, it's not too salty. Having a tasty chew will build up good positive associations with being on his bed. And remember to proof the behaviour by asking him to go to his bed from different parts of the room, whilst you're sitting, whilst you're standing, and so on.

*After stealing Frank's bed, Ragnar (a.k.a. Wussback) desperately tries to work out how to get comfortable on it. Having realised the error of his ways, the silly boy is now looking a bit forlorn.*

- **Recall (Come).** This is hard for many young dogs. The reward for not listening is often much greater than the reward for coming back to you. The first trick to establishing a solid recall is to ensure that you always get your dog's attention whenever you call his name. To do this, call his name and shove a treat in his cute little (or big) face. Do this lots of times. Before you know it, every time you call his name, he'll look to you for a treat. When he does look, mark that behaviour (click, 'yes', 'good', or whatever you prefer), and then treat him. The second trick is to only ever call your dog to you for good things and never to call him for anything he might find unpleasant. Call him when it's food time, walk time, play time, and so on. Don't call him when it's nail-cutting time, bath time, going home time, and so on (unless he finds these activities pleasant).

There's plenty of YouTube material that can help you with teaching recall. So, I'll just say that you have to remember three things to ensure recall works for you. First, make sure you are much more exciting/excitable than you have ever been when training other cues. That means better rewards and higher intensity of excitement levels when you call your dog. You might want to add movement by running/moving away with arms wide open. Secondly, don't bother calling your dog if he's in a deep sniff or overly excited playing with another puppy and you're miles away. It ain't gonna work! Wait until he's out of the deep sniff and/or disengaged from the other dog and looking around for you. Then act like an idiot and call him with a high level of excitement. Thirdly, if your dog is frightened of something and running away or is highly aroused by another dog and running towards that dog, recall isn't going to work. In those circumstances, you need to work on his fear or impulse control and keeping his arousal levels under control, before you work on his recall

- **Drop it.** There are two good ways of teaching this and one way you shouldn't. If your dog already has something in his mouth, do not just take the item from him or use intimidation or force tactics to make him release the item. This is a sure way of teaching your dog to resource guard, and before you know it, you'll be spending your hard-earned cash on a dog behaviourist to resolve that little problem.

The first way to teach your dog to drop it, or 'out', is the traditional way. Deconstructed, this approach has four component parts. Lure (with a treat), response (the drop), request (the cue), quickly followed by the reward. Sequentially: your dog has something in his mouth. You go up to him in a pleasant manner and hold a treat to the side of his mouth. As he drops the item to take the treat, you immediately say 'drop it', praise and give him the treat (the reward). In real time, everything happens almost at once. Eventually, when your dog is reliably dropping the item, then the chain of events changes slightly, with the removal of the lure. First, it is the request, then we wait for the response, followed immediately with praise and reward.

To give your dog the best chances of succeeding, make sure to use an item of low value. Also, if you're using a tuggy toy, ask for the drop BEFORE his arousal levels get to a stage where the thinking part of his brain is compromised.

Another way of teaching your dog to drop items in his mouth is slightly counterintuitive but can be effective, especially for dogs that take items and then move away from you as you approach them. This method appears to be credited to Chirag Patel, and there are several steps to the training. First, in an empty room, without anything in your dog's mouth, say the cue 'drop' and immediately throw some treats at your feet and point out/touch the treats with your finger. Proof this by repeating whilst sitting, with your coat on, whilst brushing an imaginary dirty floor, with the dog close by, the dog far away, in the kitchen, in the garden and so on. Pointing out/touching the dropped treats is important as it gets your dog accustomed to your hand being near his mouth/treats and eventually, dropped items. Once your dog is reliably running over to collect the treats with your finger touching the treats, you are ready to move on to phase two. The second stage is to introduce a toy or item of very low value to the dog. Whenever the dog even looks at the toy, say 'drop' and throw some treats on the floor by you. Your dog should run to the treats. If he doesn't, you can try reducing the value of the item on the floor, increasing the value of the treats and/or creating greater excitement and intensity when pointing out the treats. The third stage involves allowing your dog to pick up toys of ever-increasing value, and when you say drop, your dog should still drop the toy in his mouth to eat the treats. The dog may drop the toy wherever he was before running over to you, or he may bring the toy and drop it closer to the treats/you. This is where the finger touching the food and being near the dropped toy pays dividends. At this stage, when you pick up the toy, give it back to him. It's a double reward for the dog. By following this method, you will ultimately be able to pick up the dropped toy or item that you need to take from your dog.

- **Loose leash walking.** The trick to this one is to start early by acclimatising your puppy to wearing a collar/harness and lead, and rewarding him every time he is standing by your side or not pulling. At first, take only one step at a time and each time the puppy follows, reward him. Try taking a couple of steps backwards whilst facing the puppy to keep him alert and ensure his attention is on you, and then walk in a forward direction for one or two steps before rewarding him. The number of steps taken before a treat is given can be extended over time. If your puppy moves ahead or away from you, causing tension and pressure on the lead, just get his attention by calling him to you and, as he begins to follow, mark the behaviour ('good boy' or 'yes' – whatever tells him he's doing what you want) and then immediately reward him with a treat. Another thing to teach your puppy early on is to make him understand that whenever there's pressure on the leash, he needs to turn to you for a treat. Counterintuitive, I know. But what it means is that, eventually, whenever there is pressure on the leash, your dog will self-correct himself by coming back to you, or at least not moving forward. You can reinforce this behaviour by exerting a bit of pressure on the lead and then treating him. Remember to also practice loose-leash walking with added distractions – initially those that do not over-arouse him, and eventually more arousing distractions, such as other dogs. What we must not do is 'jerk' or 'snap-check' the lead or anything else that may cause the puppy/dog any distress. Remember, training has got to be undertaken through play. The effect of the above exercises is similar to when your puppy looks at you when you call his name – taught by calling his name and treating him immediately. After a while, the dog turns to you whenever his name is called.

# CHAPTER 8 – THE TALKING DOG

Dogs are learning all the time: watching us, checking out the environment, assessing situations and fashioning responses. From how we respond, they learn which behaviours get results and which behaviours don't. In his own responses, your dog is constantly communicating. Problems arise when we aren't fluent in dog language and miss or ignore our dog's signals. For example, when a dog is telling us to stay away, misunderstanding his language invariably leads to him becoming frustrated. This soon leads to problems, such as threatening, aggressive behaviours like lunging, barking, snarling, growling, snapping or even biting, which most dog owners understandably dislike and on which they seek advice from someone like me.

So, what are dogs saying to us in their language, the subtleties of which we don't always understand? A good investment and great read on the subject of body language is *Canine Body Language* by Brenda Aloff, but let's have a look at some common signals here.

## WOOF WOOF

Barking is *the* sound that distinguishes dogs from other species. When you hear a bark, you immediately think dog. Ask anyone to name an animal that barks, and 100% of people will say dog. Actually, barking is not limited to just dogs. Wolves, foxes, seals, coyotes and barking owls (sometimes called winking owls) all bark! Admittedly, the barking owl's bark sounds like a bird imitating a dog bark and is easily distinguishable from a dog's bark, but a bark it is! And the wolf? Well, wolves rarely bark and their barks are often combined with a howl or a growl. Barking is just not their preferred method of communication; it comprises only 2.4% of their vocalisations and is often brief.

Dogs, on the other hand, can bark for hours! Well, not all dogs. Every rule has an exception, and some dogs buck the trend and can't bark or only bark infrequently. The basenji is one breed that doesn't bark, though there is some evidence that it can. Generally though, basenjis yodel. There are some dogs that can and do bark, but much less so than most other dogs. These breeds include: saluki, borzoi, Glen of Imaar terrier, Australian shepherd, Shiba Inu, Irish setter, soft-coated wheaten terrier, Scottish deerhound, cavalier King Charles spaniel, bulldog, bullmastiff, and Bernese mountain dog. So, if you live in a terraced property or a flat, you might want to consider one of these dogs!

*For a quieter life – in terms of reduced barking at least!*

The majority of dog communication of course comes from the body as a whole and its component parts: the ears, eyes, tail, legs, paws, mouth and even the hair. Nevertheless, we do need to consider the dog bark and what it means. Many a neighbourly dispute has started because of a yappy dog and, sadly, many a dog has been handed into a rescue shelter because of incessant barking.

As with physical signals, barks, whines, yelps and other vocalisations have various meanings and functions. Is your dog trying to get your attention, telling you it's time to go out for a walk, warning you that the nasty postman is here again, threatening someone to stay away, soliciting play with another dog, embarking in rough-and-tumble play, or in distress?

Sonographic research demonstrates that barks sound different depending on the reason behind them. So, warning barks tend to be short and low-pitched, so deep with some dogs that the room vibrates. My Ragnar has a sufficiently hearty bark to ward off any thief who might have momentarily considered climbing over the walls and foolishly stepping inside the boundary of the property.

In fact, in the 25 years we have lived in our house, there has never been an incident, whereas the neighbours have had the odd incursion.

Barks that are intended to solicit play or attention tend to be higher in pitch and often repetitive. Where a dog feels frightened, the pitch can vary.

There's a difference between a 'stranger growl' and a 'food growl', where a dog might be guarding food in a bowl or a juicy bone or potentially a toy. In an experiment, different growls were played to a dog approaching a bone; the subject dog was certainly more hesitant in approaching on hearing the 'food growl'!

Even with somewhat inferior listening devices, in comparison with our faithful friends, most dog owners will verify that the sound of barks vary enormously depending on the circumstances. Research has demonstrated our ability to accurately guess, for example, when a dog is barking in distress. I can identify the difference between Frank's bark when he wants food and when he wants to go outside. Of course, if we were endowed with the superior hearing of dogs, we'd be able to distinguish many more types of barks and the reasons behind them. Not only can dogs hear sounds four times further away, they can hear twice as many frequencies than us. Moreover, dogs are better at differentiating sounds (they know whether it's your partner coming home or a stranger's footsteps) and pin-pointing the precise location of those sounds.

## BODY LANGUAGE

As we have discussed, even though dogs bark frequently, the majority of a dog's communication is non-verbal. The secret to accurately reading a dog's language relies on two rules. The first rule is to read signals in clusters as a suite of signals, rather than trying to interpret a single signal. This is because the same signal can mean different things depending on what else is going on and what other signals are being given off by the dog. Take for example a dog lowering his head. This can actually happen as part of a cluster of signals inviting play, part of a cluster of guarding behaviours, whilst the dog is stalking, or as an avoidance signal. The second rule is to read signals in context. A whippet might shake and shiver. If it's cold out, then it may be that he just needs a warm jacket. However, if it's warm and he's shaking, it needs to be addressed speedily as it may be due to medical reasons or it may be that the dog is shaking out of fear.

In short, rather than interpreting what a dog is trying to tell us with his eyes, ears, or the tail in isolation, a better way of understanding is to look at a cluster of signals that the dog is displaying.

# DISCOMFORT

It is said that the eyes are the windows to our souls. This equally applies to a dog's eyes. Through his eyes, a dog gives us much information about what he's really thinking and feeling. If a dog is feeling uncomfortable in a particular situation, he will give a range of signals, such as 'whale eyes' (sometimes referred to as 'half-moon eyes'). This is where the whites of the eyes can be seen and usually occurs when the dog's nose points in one direction and his eyes point in the other – often at the source of the agitation. But do look at the context and cluster of signals. Whale eyes can be seen whenever a dog looks briefly to the side. When a dog is truly uncomfortable, he will also display an accompanying cluster of signals.

Other than whale eyes, what other signals might a dog give when he is uncomfortable with a situation? The face as a whole will be somewhat tense, there will be lip licking, and the ears are likely to be drawn to the side and back. His body may be trying to lean away from the forced contact.

How often have you seen photographs posted on social media of children hugging the family dog in the name of cuteness? However, judging by the body language of the dogs being hugged, some of them are certainly not finding it cute at all. Having said that, some dogs evidently don't mind and some even quite enjoy being hugged. Each dog should be treated as an individual.

In any event, why are we so hell bent on hugging our dogs? It's probably all down to us anthropomorphising them. Most of us like hugging each other. Children love being hugged. So we apply human logic and leap to the conclusion that dogs must also like being hugged. Actually, devoid of arms as such, not much hugging goes on in the dog world. Nor, for that matter, does patting. The mother only strokes and licks her puppy with her tongue, she doesn't pat or hug. It's a bugbear of mine (which appears to have multiplied exponentially since hitting half a century). I get very irritated when people stroke and apply hearty pats on Ragnar's flanks or chest. Sometimes the patting is so hard, I let out a growl under my breath on behalf of my poor dog.

*Comfortable and relaxed dog body language.*

VS

*Dogs showing anxiety and stress.*

Cute? Ears down, half-moon eyes, head turned away to avoid eye contact, yawning… A cluster of signals.

Of course, it's not just hugging, but a wide variety of situations that may cause a dog to feel uncomfortable. A dog that is of a nervous or anxious disposition may easily become overwhelmed by any social pressure. Often the discomfort can be seen when members of the public feel they know better and, on seeing a dog that is a little shy, impose themselves even further by reaching out to befriend him. Nothing is more likely to exacerbate the situation and cause even more discomfort. In these situations you're likely to see further signs of discomfort, including the dog averting his gaze rather than looking at the person, yawning, lifting one paw and leaning backwards slightly, cringing, lowering his whole body and, under extreme discomfort, urinating.

## COMFORTABLE/RELAXED

If the dog is feeling comfortable in a situation, the signals will be very different. The eyes will be soft, not looking away, not squinted, not hard, staring or eyeballing (as you might do if you were furious with someone and were signalling your intention to inflict serious harm!). Additionally, a comfortable dog is likely to lean into a person touching him, there is unlikely to be any tension in his body and his tail is likely to be gently wagging. The ears are likely to be floppy whilst the mouth will be relaxed and open, with a lolling tongue.

*Relaxed with a loose facial expression.*

# STAY AWAY/WARNING

There are a number of situations where a dog may not want you or another dog near him. One of the most common is when a dog is in possession of an item he considers valuable. This could be a chew, toy, place or even a person.

The reason behind dogs guarding items is founded in basic dog law: what is in my mouth or in my vicinity is MINE! This law is clear and understood by all dogs, but not always by owners. So owners often end up taking items away from dogs by using force, which just teaches the dog that you are competition, and therefore someone against whom guarding behaviours need to be escalated in order to enforce dog law. More on this in Chapter 12.

The other thing that is very clear is the language used to remind any other dog that might have any doubts as to the fine print of the dog law, such as the size of the vicinity. But whilst this language is clear to all dogs, it is not always clear to owners. Well, in any event, it certainly wasn't clear enough to one client, who instructed me after having been bitten by his dog six times in the space of 14 days due to resource guarding signals being unrecognised. So, I gathered a range of photos of dogs warning others to stay away during resource guarding to support a verbal explanation of resource guarding signals for the client.

Signals during resource guarding tend to escalate in intensity from 'errr, this is mine – stop there and don't come any closer' to 'you've had several warnings – come one step closer and I'm going to sink my teeth into you, since you're leaving me with no other choice!' A dog displaying such signals will initially become stiff or still, perhaps followed by a direct stare or eyes wide open. The head might become lowered. Sometimes, a dog might look at you out of the top of his eyes with his nose pointing towards the resource. Staring at you is a very clear sign of guarding behaviour, as opposed to looking away from you, which is a sign of deference. Don't try to intimidate your dog by staring back and continuing with your approach. You may be successful in making him submit on an occasion or two, but I promise you, unless there are some negotiating signals from your dog (such as blinking or averting his gaze) you will get bitten eventually, or the various problems that come with force-based tactics will arise. If the dog's pupils become dilated, this is a clear physiological response to adrenaline being released into the system. Your dog is now stressed, fearful and potentially about to fly into a rage and bite.

When not in a resource guarding situation, when a dog wants to avoid another dog or person, he'll start with submission signals. The progression from 'please go away, I'm not comfortable here' to biting might go something like this: yawning, blinking, nose licking > turning head away > turning body away, sitting pawing > walking away > creeping, ear back > standing crouched, tail tucked under > lying down, leg up > stiffening up, staring, growling > snapping > biting.[13]

The mouth is also an area that signals emotions. Reading signals emanating from the mouth can be difficult with hirsute dogs, but it's easier with dogs like Labradors. When stressed, the dog's mouth will become tight and closed, almost making a C shape – the opposite of a relaxed dog with lips pulled back and a lolling tongue. And so, the severity of the warning signals continue to increase. Have the lips become raised, is the snout now wrinkled, and have the teeth been bared? A growl might then follow, and if you persist, the growl might be followed by an air snap. Even the greenest of beginners will have by now retreated. But evidently not Cesar Millan, who in one TV clip didn't read any of the many signals a Labrador gave him whilst resource guarding his bowl of food. The only logical step left for a dog in such a situation is the final signal. The bite, as was inflicted on Millan.

*C- shaped mouth.*

13      Quain, A. 'Three things I learned: the neurophysiology of canine anxiety.' *Small Animal Talk.* Available from http://www.smallanimaltalk.com/2014/03/three-things-i-learned-neurophysiology.html

# THE TAIL

The tail has so many different movements that it is almost worthy of studying as a subject in its own right. As always, any movement of the tail needs to be read as part of a cluster of other body signals, but by golly does it have a huge vocabulary. And rightly so – dogs are highly tuned to movement.

Sure, a dog's tail goes up and down. Depending on the other signals being given, a tail held up high can suggest a confident disposition, or that the dog is agitated, or prepared and ready to confront the source of his interest. A high tail also has the added benefit of allowing other dogs to more easily smell the high-tailed dog's odour. That odour gives the other dogs some very useful information. A human's six million nose sensory receptors are dwarfed by a dog's, which can be north of 300 million – enough for them to accurately establish if someone is a diabetic and whether their sugar levels are too high or if they're about to go into a hypoglycaemic attack. This super-nose is likely to glean many more facts from sniffing another dog's rear than we might listening to the 7 p.m. Channel 4 News.

A lowered tail communicates that the dog is not so confident and not a threat. A tail tucked under communicates that the dog is even less confident and perhaps feeling fearful or stressed. Sometimes a dog can exhibit higher levels of submission by tucking its whole back end under itself.

A relaxed and hanging tail suggests the dog is fairly neutral about the encounter, being neither over-confident nor concerned in any way. Curious about something? That's when the tail is likely to be held straight out.

*Look at a cluster of signals. The tail is up and wagging stiffly. Threatening. Is the danger backed up by the ears and a direct stare?*

And then, of course, there's the classic case of a dog's tail going side to side. 'The tail's wagging so he must be friendly', I hear people say. Yes, if it's hanging in a relaxed, neutral position and swaying gently – but that's not the only wag you'll see. A tail that is held high or vertically and wagging stiffly and fast or almost trembling can be a real threat. In fact, the faster the wag, the more emotionally charged the situation, suggesting high arousal or excitement levels.

In addition to the tail's many movements, the eyes and ears carry out all sorts of acrobatics. And let's not forget about the hair on your dog's back. This also rises depending on his arousal levels. If the raised hackles (piloerection) don't revert to normal soon after an introduction to another dog, this can be a sign of concern, as it could lead to potential aggression.

*Ragnar looks nervous because he is leaning backwards, but the fast wagging tail suggests he will put up a fight if the pony persists in approaching.*

A fast-wagging, low tail is indicative of a dog that is anxious, submissive or fearful. You might be familiar with this one if you've ever come downstairs and noticed a chewed and damaged carpet!

In 2013, a team of neuroscientists at an Italian university found that tails also wag in different directions depending on the situation.[14]

14    Siniscalchi, M., Lusito, R., Vallortigara, G., and Quaranta, Q. (2013) 'Seeing left- or right-asymmetric tail wagging produces different emotional responses in dogs.' PMID: 24184108 DOI: 10.1016/j.cub.2013.09.027

If a dog sees his owner or a person or another dog that he knows, he's more likely to wag his tail predominantly to the right (our left, if we're looking at the dog head on). But if it's someone, something or a dog they don't know or would rather avoid, they tend to wag their tail more to the left!

Let us not forget the windmill tail and the tail that draws furious arcs! Frank is a master at this, and my daughter has mooted harnessing his windmill-tail proclivity to produce environmentally friendly electricity, particularly in times of high fuel costs. This type of wagging is reserved for those occasions when the dog is so excited the tail seems to want to do everything at once; maybe when your dog hasn't seen you for a few days, or in the case of Frank, every time he sees my daughter (or anyone for that matter).

The movement I'm not particularly keen on? No movement at all – especially if it's accompanied by other aggressive body signals. The dog may just be saying 'make my day, punk!' The lack of movement is often the stillness before a storm. It may signal a happy storm, where the dog is just about to activate 'zoomies mode' (frenetic random activity periods) and go crazy with happiness for a few minutes. On the other hand, it might signal a very unpleasant storm. Unless you back away very calmly, offering all the calming signals you can muster, you might be about to get bitten.

With the tail alone having 12 more moves than me on a dance floor, certain breeds that have unconventional tails face challenges in communicating with other dogs and us. For instance pugs, Boston terriers and other such breeds, which have tightly curled tails. Additionally, whippets, through much selective breeding, have tails that are curled and tucked under their hind legs. Beagles generally hold their tails straight out. These tail traits might lead to misinterpretation at a distance, even by other dogs, and by us if looked at in isolation. Even more reason to read signals in clusters and in context.

## GENERAL SIGNS OF STRESS

In addition to some of the signals set out above, there are various others that can signify that dog is feeling stress, causing the release of cortisol.

Brenda Aloff illustrates with photographs the following list of signals, some of which your dog might display when stressed:

whining, yawning, lip licking/tongue flicking, 'hard eye' or stare, avoiding eye contact, one front paw raised, grinning, lip curling, furrowed brow, clinging to owner/trying to 'climb' the owner, shaking, tense ears or ears pinned back, panting, tongue way out or spatulate tongue, freezing, shaking off (as when wet) and not taking treats. So, look out for these signals, and if your dog does display any of them, calmly and sympathetically manage his environment to help him escape the stressors.

## PLAY

Play can be a very rough-and-tumble activity, with much growling, biting and other signals that may occasionally be mistaken as aggression or inappropriate play.

*"I'll take you both on!!" (walkwagplay)*

To assess whether play is taking place rather than aggression, it is useful to remember the acronyms **BRIDLE** and **MARS.** If BRIDLE or MARS behaviours are present, play is afoot and you don't need to get involved. First, let's look at **BRIDLE:**

**B** – You will remember that predatory motor pattern we discussed in Chapter 2:

Eye>Stalk>Chase>Grab-bite>Grab-Kill>Dissect>Consume. Well, when a dog is engaged in play, this **behaviour** sequence becomes jumbled up. So you may get a grab-bite and then chase.

**R** – Various behaviours will be **repeated** again and again during play, whether this be nudging another dog with hind quarters or pouncing.

**I** – During play, a dog will perform **incomplete** behaviours. He might go in for a neck bite but stop before he actually makes contact.

**D** – The final injurious motor pattern of 'kill-bite' is always **dropped** in a play situation.

**L** – When playing, a dog's face is soft and **loose** along with the rest of the body.

**E** – Body movements tend to be **exaggerated**.

And then there's **MARS:**

**M** – **Meta communication.** This is how dogs tell each other that they mean no harm. You'll have heard of the play bow, which is one such signal. The play bow says, 'please can I attack you or chase you' or 'please come and chase me' – but all in fun. You'll have seen the play bow. The dog lowers his front legs but keeps his rump in the air with the tail hanging loose. Once given, play won't actually start until the receiver acknowledges it with his own meta-communication response. Often, it's not even a full play bow. During play, there might be a quick lowering of the body or head – especially amongst good friends. These truncated signals are often missed by us, but clear enough to the other dog. Then there's the prey bow – same as the play bow, except the tail is up. This is a slightly different proposition. 'Mate, just to let you know that this is all in fun, but beware because I'm about to pounce on you!!'

**A** – **Activity shifts.** Play activities will stop and start on a regular basis. There will be a period of mad play then a period of the dogs just going about their own business doing not very much, or they may just stand next to each other for a few seconds. Then the play will restart. As activities stop, you may also see your dog shaking his whole body as if shaking off excess water after a swim. This means the dog is coming off an adrenaline rush, initially released due to high arousal levels or anxiety. It acts as a signal to the other dog that play needs to cease momentarily. Before play restarts, there are likely to be more meta communications to restart play.

*An emotional encounter –*
*play got too rough, over-excitement or anxiety.*

**R** – **Reversal of roles.** You will often find one dog initially doing all the attacking and biting whilst the other dog is in a submissive position on his back whilst being mauled. Then the next minute, roles are reversed and the submissive dog is all of a sudden the dominant one and administering all the mauling.

**S** – Dogs will **self-handicap** themselves during play in a way which is covered by the E in BRIDLE – with exaggerated movements. It's all about biting and pouncing in such a way that inhibits their actions, thus ensuring they don't hurt their play partner.

## MISINTERPRETING BODY LANGUAGE

Due to selective breeding, it is sometimes difficult to understand a dog's language unless signals are read in clusters and in context. We've already discussed how it might be difficult for a dog with, for example, a curly tail to convey submission with the use of his tail. Similarly, dogs with large protruding eyes might be misunderstood by people and possibly other dogs as conveying dominant and aggressive signals. And what about hirsute dogs? Might we miss a curled up lip or bared teeth, warning us to stay away? Is that why small, designer breeds are often more aggressive[15] than larger, more wolf-like breeds that have the capacity to display the full repertoire of body signals? Or do small dogs show aggression more frequently because their owners just don't allow them to practise being a dog, and pick them up at the first sign of another larger approaching dog? Or is it because owners of small breeds forgive their indiscretions because they are regarded as cute? Bit of everything, I expect.

---

15      Mikkola, S., Salonen, M., Puurunen, J., Hakanen, E., Sulkama, S., Araujo, C. and Lohi, H. (2021) 'Aggressive behaviour is affected by demographic, environmental and behavioural factors in purebred dogs.' *Scientific Reports*, vol. 11, Article number: 9433.

# CHAPTER 9 –
# WHY DOES MY DOG DO THAT?
# DISPELLING SOME MYTHS

Periodically, during my dog behaviour seminars, I split attendees into small groups for break-out sessions and pose them questions that from time to time occupy a dog owner's mind. The responses vary. Some bizarre, some correct. And my favourite? Those responses that, in the absence of existing research, offer a credible explanation for a particular behaviour or question. So, let's look at some of the questions that might have found their way into your mind and clear up any misapprehensions.

## WHY DOES MY DOG
## STARE AT ME WHEN HE POOPS?

There's been no research on this point, so your explanation may be as valid as the next person's. Most people tend to agree that this is chiefly for protection. Namely, that the dog is in a vulnerable position during eliminations and looks to you to ensure there are no lurking dangers. There may be something in this protection theory. Whilst your dog can probably smell any potential dangers from a considerable distance away, he may look to you whilst on a poop break as a way to communicate that it's your turn to take over sentry duties for a while. The other reason may be to keep an eye on you, to ensure you don't disappear from sight and, if you do, to know where you went so he can catch up with you.

However, there may be another reason: that we have conditioned him to look at us during his potty-training years. How many times did you watch your dog when he was first learning to eliminate outdoors, just so that you could make a big fuss of him when he did pee or poop? I confess, I still make a fuss of my dog and Frank when they go about their business, and they're aged four and two respectively. So now, they're used to looking at me and waiting for my praise when they do go.

*Good boy, Ragnar.*

## WHY DOES MY DOG CIRCLE BEFORE GOING FOR A POOP?

Lots of theories here and a little bit of research. Some theorise that it's a means of checking for any critters underfoot prior to assuming the position. Some argue that it may be a means of leaving additional scent on the ground via the dog's paws. Certainly, dogs do release pheromones from special glands in between their toes. I'm not entirely convinced by the latter explanation. I should imagine the scent from the anal glands and excrement would be more than sufficient to leave a marker. However, it is true that different glands communicate different scents, so there may be something in this theory.

Another argument is that the dog is trying to smooth out the ground to give himself a nice clean place to do his business. This really isn't borne out by anecdotal evidence of dogs (including my own) that do their best work in tall grasses, without the circling ritual. Very discreet, in my view.

There is another theory that suggests dogs circle to stimulate their intestines to prepare for the elimination.

Whilst all these theories pose credible interpretations, on balance, my view is that circling is chiefly a way of securing a good footing and to check that there are no dangers around whilst they are in a rather vulnerable position.

Now, there has been some interesting research on the matter of eliminations. A 2013 study checked out 70 dogs going about their business. 37 breeds were involved. 2000 craps and 6000 pees later, the findings suggested that dogs are going about their business in a north-south magnetic axis, and will avoid facing east or west.[16] But these dogs were let loose on open ground, without the added stimulation of lampposts or walls – not always the case in the real world. If there is some truth in this alignment, science still has no idea why dogs might align themselves so. Do they do it consciously or does it just make them feel good? No one knows!

## WHY DOES MY DOG EAT POOP?

There's a lot less guesswork and theorising on this issue and a fair bit of science and research. Firstly, if your dog is a poop eater (a coprophage), you're not alone! A 2012 study of 3000 dogs, led by Dr B Hart, found that 16% of dogs had been caught eating poop more than five times and 24% had been observed eating poop at least once.[17] The research also found that coprophagia is more common amongst females (and least likely amongst intact males), greedy dogs that steal food, and in multi-dog households. It also found that 85% of dogs do not eat their own excrement.

So, what's it all about? Why do dogs eat poop? There are several reasons:

**Medical related reasons** – These include: a medical condition causing an increase in appetite, a nutritionally or calorie deficient diet, malabsorption syndrome or even certain medications, such as steroids.

**Emotional reasons** – The dog may be being kept in isolation, rather than in a social circle with their owner, which is so craved

---

16      Hart et al. (2013) 'Dogs are sensitive to small variations of the Earth's magnetic field.' *Frontiers in Zoology*, 10:80. Available from: http://www.frontiersinzoology.com/content/10/1/80

17      Hart, B. L. (2012) 'Behavioral defences in animals against pathogens and parasites: parallels with pillars of medicine in humans.' *Philosophical Transactions of the Royal Society B* 366, pp.3406 –3417.

by dogs; being confined in small spaces; suffering from anxiety, if the dog has been previously punished for soiling indoors. The latter particularly may cause the dog to hide the evidence by eating it, to avoid further punishment.

**Instinctual reasons** – In the absence of human intervention, we know mothers will clean up their puppy's excrement by eating it for the first few weeks of birth. It's the only way of keeping the 'den' clean. This instinctual activity may stay with some females, as they continue the behaviour into adulthood. Puppies naturally copy the mother's behaviour and, again, whilst most puppies grow out of it, it is easy to understand the root of the behaviour.

**Behavioural reasons** – There may occasionally be cases of dogs eating poop because they are not getting the attention they need. A dog eating poop is more likely to be given what he deems to be a sufficient amount of attention and, furthermore, it can turn into a game for him!

## WHY DOES MY DOG DESTROY FURNITURE?

**Exploration** – For puppies, chewing is normal. And when devoid of hands and opposable thumbs, exploration is done through the nose and mouth! Chewing is also extremely pleasurable for the puppy, as it releases feel-good chemicals, including endorphins. This chewing behaviour stops once the puppy has been taught what is and isn't on the menu.

**Separation Anxiety** – Destruction, especially at doors and windows, is a common behaviour when dogs become stressed due to separation.

**Fabric Sucking** – For puppies, the teat is a great source of nutrition and comfort. Where mothers do not allow their puppies to suckle, especially during the anxiety period, those puppies may resort to sucking on fabrics, e.g., blankets, cushions and so on. Furthermore, during puppyhood, dogs are given soft toys which they mouth and suck, treating the toy as a pacifier and often falling asleep whilst sucking. There may be other reasons: teething, the taste of the blanket, canine compulsive disorder and anxiety. Fabric sucking can develop into a need to continue sucking other fabrics on sofas and can act as a gateway behaviour to destructive behaviours.

*Bed for sale! I'd prefer if you can collect before my owners get home.*
*Yours sincerely, Frank.*

**Nutritional deficiencies** – As with coprophagia, destruction and eating non-foods (pica) may be due to some nutritional deficiency, which your vet will be able to test for.

**Poorly enriched life** – As has been well documented, bored dogs that have a poorly enriched life, including lack of mental stimulation and insufficient exercise, resort to destructive behaviours to occupy their time and satisfy their artistic bent whilst the owner is away.

## WHY DOES MY DOG SHAKE WHEN NOT WET?

There may be many reasons behind this behaviour. 'Wet shaking' in the mornings may just be a primal behaviour – namely, the need to shake off any critters that may be clinging on. Alternatively, it may just be part of the dog's morning routine. Sometimes, it may just be a head shake for the sake of a head shake. However, excessive head shaking should be taken seriously as it normally points to a medical condition, such as an ear infection.

There is one set of circumstances that always makes a dog wet shake. This is when the dog has had an intense emotional encounter that causes him to release adrenaline, and also cortisol, if it was a stressful experience. Consequently, the wet shaking is a clear signal of a dog coming off an adrenaline rush and shaking off pent-up stress.

# WHY DOES MY DOG STEAL CLOTHES?

There are three main reasons for this. First, clothes contain copious amounts of your pheromones and general aroma – even more so when unwashed, and even better if it's underwear. Pheromones released through our apocrine glands are primarily located in our genitalia, nipple and armpit areas. These pheromones tell the puppy about your mood, whether you're menstruating and even whether you've had sex. I'm not suggesting that a dog can necessarily interpret the meaning of these different states, but it will certainly know that you are in a different state. Licking and chewing the stolen items actually helps release more odour.

Secondly, they're a jolly good chew or something to suck on – puppies particularly find this comforting. In addition, it's a natural instinct. Certain types of breeds might find soft, furry clothing more appealing than other breeds as it may remind them of feathers and fur.

Thirdly, it can become a game. As soon as their underwear is taken, most people will make a huge fuss and try to retrieve the stolen item. This very soon becomes a great game for the puppy! Well done – you've just made the underwear even more valuable to your dog.

A final underlying factor behind clothes stealing may simply be that the dog is bored, particularly with his toys that are constantly accessible to him. Dogs are neophiles. So, change toys around and ensure he's getting plenty of mental stimulation.

*Frank likes mummy's socks.*

# WHY DOES MY DOG ROLL AROUND IN STRONG SMELLS?

Again, lots of theories here but not much by way of hard scientific research. Ethologists suggest several reasons for this. First, dogs may want to mask their own scent so that they can better creep up on prey or make it harder for predators to detect them. Secondly, it may be a way of dogs marking the area as their own territory. Thirdly, covering themselves with the smell may be a means of taking messages contained in the smell back to the pack or social group (us). Some researchers suggest that dogs may roll around in others' smells to create a feeling of group unity. Namely, if your dog is rolling around in your dirty laundry, he may just be trying to smell like you.

# HOW DOES NATURE AFFECT A DOG'S CHARACTER?

We have covered this in previous chapters, to some extent. Different dog breeds are apt to act differently in any given situation. A gun dog, such as a spaniel, is more likely to wander away from his owner and roam the woodland walk compared to a guarding breed such as a German shepherd, which is likely to stay close to his owner. This is thanks to selective breeding over many years.

However, thresholds are not only informed by breeding but also vary due to a dint of fate. Dogs can be born with a particular trait. Some are born introverts – they're often the anxious ones. Some are born extroverts – they're often quite demanding of attention and are the first ones to say hello to a dog or person across the field! Studies by Marc Bekoff show that wolves and wild coyotes develop 'wildly' different personalities by the age of three weeks[18] – well before any contact with the outside world. Many scientists also argue that based on these inherent personalities and levels of confidence, some dogs are naturally more dominant when it comes to interactions and establishing relationships and rankings with other dogs.

# DO DOGS HAVE A SENSE OF SELF?

---

18    Bekoff, M. and Wells, M. C. (1986). 'Social ecology and behavior of coyotes.' *Advances in the Study of Behavior*, 16, pp.251–338.

The traditional way to determine whether an animal recognises himself is the mirror test, developed by Gordon Gallup. In this test, a coloured mark is placed on the forehead of an animal, which is given access to a mirror. Those that have a sense of self checked out the mark. Other than humans, who pass with flying colours, not many animals pass the test. Species that have recognised themselves include the great apes, the Eurasian magpie, orcas, dolphins and the cleaner wrasse. Dogs, cats, monkeys, giant pandas and sea lions all fail the test.

However, there is now agreement amongst scientists that the Gallup test is not the only method of assessing self-awareness. The test is of limited value when applied to animals that use olfaction as their main source of learning, such as dogs. Using olfaction tests, a number of experiments show that dogs recognise themselves through an awareness of whether a particular smell is theirs or not. In the smell test, dogs spent less time sniffing their own pee than other dogs' pee.

*On the left, a still taken from a video in which Frank watched himself in the mirror and growled at the image for over 30 seconds until he came to realise there was no danger and walked off. On the right, Ragnar. Does he recognise there's a mark on his forehead and that there's something different about himself? Not according to research.*

# ARE DOGS COLOUR-BLIND?

I have heard many people say that dogs only see in black and white. The truth of the matter is that they don't really see red, yellow and orange very well. Nor are dogs particularly good at seeing colour shades containing any of those colours, such as pink and purple. All this is down to the fact that whilst people have three colour receptors in each eye, perceiving red, blue and green wavelengths, dogs only have two, perceiving blue and a greenish-yellow wavelength! So, dogs see blue and green colours the best, as well as various shades of grey, black and white. But it seems not to hinder dogs at all. What we need to keep in mind is that humans are primarily visual in their learning, followed by hearing, touch and sense of smell. Dogs on the other hand are almost the opposite. Sense of smell is their primary learning machine, followed by hearing and, finally, sight.

Whilst smell is enough for dogs to establish where things are, sight is also important, and this sense evolved because most of what wolves eat runs away or is camouflaged – and camouflage is exposed by movement. Sight helps wolves to identify the precise location of prey. Further, their prey is often active at dusk or dawn, so they developed eyes sensitive in low light. So, colour is not hugely important in the dog world.

# ARE DOGS STRANGERS ONCE SEPARATED FROM THEIR LITTERMATES?

This is a tricky one. There is much anecdotal evidence of dogs that have been ecstatic to see their littermate after many years of separation. Bearing in mind a dog's powerful sense of smell, stories of instant recognition are quite believable. However, there is not much scientific research on the matter. Some researchers believe that for littermates kept together up to the age of 16 weeks (rare), there is a high probability that they will recognise each other, even after a couple of years.

On the other hand, a Belfast University study confirmed that whilst after two years of separation 76% of dogs recognised the smell of their mother and vice versa, the evidence for recognition of littermates after two years was inconclusive. The anecdotal evidence may have simply confused recognition with two dogs that just instantly got on.

## DOES CASTRATION STOP A DOG FROM BEING AGGRESSIVE?

During aggression in intact males, testosterone is definitely present, as aggression stimulates testosterone production. So, there's definitely a correlation. But that's not the same as saying testosterone actually causes aggression. In tests, testosterone was administered to a group of men at higher levels than to a control group; the experiment did not prove that the additional testosterone caused increased aggression in the first group. However, since testosterone increases confidence and optimism and decreases anxiety and fear, the absence of testosterone due to castration can increase anxiety and fear. The lethal cocktail of anxiety and fear is often at the root of aggression. So, castration and the ensuing reduction in testosterone could actually cause aggression rather than reduce it.

Research tends to point to the fact that the more experience a male has of being aggressive prior to castration, the more likely he is to continue being aggressive. So, castration could reduce aggression, but that would only be in cases where the dog isn't or doesn't become anxious or fearful as a result of the absence of testosterone and where there is no prior experience of aggression through social learning.

Whilst we're on the subject of castration, what about spaying? After all, female dogs also have a bitey end! Should we consider spaying them if they show aggression? As we are aware, there can be non-hormonal reasons for aggression. For example, fear or physical pain (unlinked to any pain caused by increased soreness due to being in oestrus) need to be addressed first.

Ovaries make most of the oestrogen and progesterone and also play a part in testosterone production. Consequently, spaying reduces the production of only these hormones and stops the ovulation cycle.

The balance of the evidence below suggests spaying may increase the risks of aggression:

• Progesterone inhibits aggressive behaviour in females. Therefore, lower levels of progesterone after a spaying may have the opposite effect.

- A study suggests that spaying may increase the risk not only of aggression towards owners, but also of long-term problems including diabetes mellitus, various cancers, hypothyroidism, etc. These conditions may impact a spayed dog's homeostasis and control of the stress response towards her owners. However, it was found that there were differences between breeds and size of dog in terms of the impact of spaying on the various conditions referred to above.

- Canine Cognitive Dysfunction can increase anxiety. Spayed females are more likely to show signs of CCD than intact females. In turn, increased anxiety could activate the fear system (p. 29) more readily, leading to fear-linked aggression towards owners.

- Another study found that spayed females tend to be more fearful and more anxious.

- There is evidence that after spaying, there is a 33% increase in sensitivity to touch/handling. This could increase reactivity and therefore aggressive behaviours when touched.

- Research has shown that spaying contributes to increased aggression, stimulus reactivity and increased 'dominance' aggression towards family members, particularly where spaying is carried out on puppies under the age of 12 months that were already showing some aggression.

However, you may have had different experiences. There is research that suggests spaying may decrease the risk of aggression for the following reasons:

- Research points to lower levels of cortisol (which has been linked to stress situations, aggression and fear), testosterone and progesterone one week after spaying. Furthermore, it showed higher serotonin levels (linked to lower aggression) four weeks after spaying.

- Elevations in oestrogen affect dogs in a number of ways including becoming unpredictable, anxious and experiencing physical discomfort. This means that the fear system may become more readily activated, leading to aggression motivated by the desire to avoid the negative affect of fear. Spaying potentially decreases these levels.

- Females are biologically less prone to aggression than males, and one reason for this may be the relatively low levels of testosterone in females. Reduction of testosterone by spaying would potentially further reduce any testosterone-fuelled aggression.

# CHAPTER 10 –
# INTRODUCTION TO INTRODUCTIONS

Dog owners normally instruct dog behaviourists because their dog is displaying behaviours that have started to cause problems. By this I mean:

1. Problems for the owners. This may include pulling on the lead, nipping, jumping up or just generally not doing what is appropriate in the human world or perhaps is acceptable in the owner's household.

2. Problems for others. For example, a dog's behaviour towards another dog may be disproportionate to the stimulus. The dog sees another dog walking by, and suddenly mild-mannered Fido turns into a monster baring its teeth, snarling and frothing at the mouth.

3. Problems for the dog, especially when he can't function normally through fears or phobias. Perhaps a certain stimulus leads to constant stress, which can, of course, affect learning and cause medical problems.

These problems, in turn, lead to a range of consequences, which can be minor or far more serious, including injury.

In Chapter 4 we considered the many factors that can cause psychological behavioural issues and the ensuing behavioural 'problems' referred to above. These factors include:

1. Lack of proper and early socialisation.

2. Traumatic experiences.

3. Medical issues.

4. Genetic issues.

5. Punishment-based training methods.

6. Major changes and upheavals in a dog's life – this causes stress, which is not good for the dog.

But there's an area of a dog's life that doesn't get the coverage it deserves but can equally lead to serious consequences if not managed carefully. This area is all about how the dog experiences introductions to other animals. Specifically, situations involving:

- An existing dog and the arrival of a new baby.
- An existing dog and the arrival of a new animal/puppy.
- Existing toddlers/children and the arrival of a new dog.

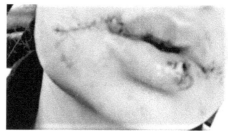

# INAPPROPRIATE INTRODUCTIONS AND THEIR CONSEQUENCES

So, let's avoid the scenes depicted in these photos and look at some dos and, very importantly, the don'ts when it comes to initial introductions.

However, before we talk about the best way to handle specific introductions, there are four main things to bear in mind:

1. Introductions are a process, not a one-time event. Think about how we make friends or develop relationships in our lives. Just like

us, it takes time and many positive experiences for dogs to build relationships and start to trust and see other animals as friends and part of their social group.

2. This process must proceed at the dog's pace, not yours. Two variables here. First, your current dog's proclivities. There may be one dog in your family who may take months to build a solid relationship and another who is ready to share his favourite chew with his new best friend within 20 minutes of the initial meeting. The other variable is the personality of the newcomer.

3. Don't apply human logic to your dog. You may go weak at the knees and instantly fall in love with a new puppy or kitten or baby, but don't expect your dog to do that. Dogs see things slightly differently. Small things like a cat move quickly, and might cause predatory motor patterns to kick in – especially if you've got a greyhound. A terrier may have a low threshold to noticing movement and perceiving it as a threat, leading to undesired consequences.

Going back to basics, how many people socialise their puppy to babies and other animals during that crucial, very sensitive 5–12 week period? And unless your dog has been constantly exposed to puppies, he is more than likely to sense trouble when a new one shows up. Also, with a new puppy or an interspecies interaction, the normal rules of play between two dogs go out the window. There's no invitation to play, no acceptance of the play invitation, and potential failure to recognise signals requesting play to stop. A heady mix for potential trouble.

4. Keep introductions short and sweet. Extended sessions have the potential of causing over-arousal, which in turn compromises the thinking part of the brain.

# EXISTING DOG – NEW BABY

There are three fundamental points to remember when a new baby is involved.

1. Dogs are social animals and want to be part of your social circle. This is crucial to a dog's emotional wellbeing, and its impact on your dog mustn't be underestimated. So, please don't exclude him from the fun and the joys that a new arrival will bring by isolating him in a separate room of the house or behind a gate all the time.

2. Having said that, the second thing to remember is that dogs are instinctual animals. Regardless of how well you might know

your dog, he shouldn't be left unsupervised with the baby for the reasons we've already touched on.

3. Finally, as with all introductions, *take small steps*. The aim is to achieve our long-term goal: to let him know that the baby is part of his social circle, that he need not be troubled by her presence and the general smells and noises emanating from her, and that actually, the youngster is a great playmate and far more fun than the adults in the house.

With the above in mind, there's a list of things to do, and of equal importance, a list of things to avoid.

## DOS BEFORE ARRIVAL

What we're trying to do here is reduce the extent of the upheaval to the dog's life, which can cause psychological and behavioural issues.

* Buy the baby equipment and set up the baby's room well before the happy arrival. When you've done that, allow your dog to explore the baby's room, equipment, pushchair and so forth on a regular basis.

*Frank, slowly getting used to the pram –*
*with lots of treats to form good associations.*

* Habituate your dog to the new noises that he's going to experience when the baby arrives, such as babies crying. When I was habituating Frank to baby cries five months before the arrival of my first granddaughter, his initial reaction was to bark at the noise. You

don't want to add that into the mix when you've just had a baby! Also, now would be a good time to ask friends to let you have unwashed clothes from their babies to help your dog to experience new baby smells. And finally, if your dog is anything like Frank and likes to pick up socks, underpants, toys and anything else lying around the floor, it might be a good idea to get him used to leaving things alone, particularly if he has any resource guarding tendencies.

• Finally, try to introduce changes you feel are unavoidable, prior to the arrival – e.g., shorter walks, less attention, or later wake-ups.

# DOS AFTER ARRIVAL

• When your baby has arrived, leave an item of baby's clothing or muslin in the dog's bed so he can get used to her smell.

• Allow your dog to calmly investigate and sniff the baby's feet, legs and body whilst she's safely in your arms.

• For dogs with very gentle mouths, put a treat on the blanket covering the baby's feet and let him take that treat.

• Feel free to resort to complementary therapies such as Bach flower remedies. There's a fair amount of anecdotal evidence that certain remedies like mimulus, Rescue Remedy, appropriate flower essences added to your dog's water, and synthetic dog-appeasing pheromones will help to reduce any anxiety and help him be calm around the baby.

• Regularly remind your dog of the behaviour that is required of him when he is interacting with the baby. No pawing, jumping up or getting overexcited. But we do want the dog to sit or calmly lie down next to the baby. Treat him with some super-high-value treats each time he and the baby meet and whenever he is calm and gentle around her.

• As already mentioned, allow your dog to be part of the room. This should be done at safe distances, though. For example, the baby should be in your arms or a highchair while the dog is on his mat tucking into a tasty chew (unless he has resource guarding tendencies).

• The triangle. Practice creating distance between yourself, the baby and the dog on a regular basis, forming the three points of an imaginary triangle. To ensure safety, the dog can be secured on a leash, the end of which can be attached to a hook on the wall or under a sofa leg.

- In due course, hold the baby's hand in your hand when stroking the dog.
- At all times keep a look out for any signal from the dog that suggests he is uncomfortable. Your dog is going to be exposed to a plethora of new sights, sounds and smells. Body language suggesting the dog is uncomfortable means he has become overwhelmed.
- Do try to keep any changes in your dog's routines to a minimum and, as already mentioned, make unavoidable changes before the happy arrival.

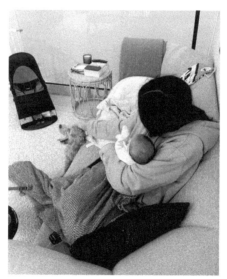

*Frank taking his time –*
*slow acclimatisation is the fastest way to become good friends.*

# DON'TS

- Force any interaction between the baby and the dog. Instead, allow the dog to come to the baby and instigate with a sniff or other suitably gentle interaction.
- Keep the dog away in a separate room (e.g., using a baby gate or tethered) whilst you and the baby are in a different room, other than for short periods to help the dog acclimatise to being comfortable in your absence.
- Tell the dog off if he makes a mistake near the baby. We do not want him to associate the baby with something unpleasant.
- Be anxious about the introduction. Your anxiety will rub off on the dog. Practise remaining calm. You can be vigilant without freaking out. Remember, dogs become very familiar with the way we normally act. You becoming anxious changes the way you normally move, your breathing increases, your heartbeat quickens, you release cortisol and adrenaline. These changes will be noticed by your dog and he may interpret the changes as meaning something is not quite right. Consequently, he will also act differently from normal.
- Allow unsupervised access to the baby's room/cot or leave the baby and dog unsupervised. This is worth reiterating. All too often a crawling baby may reach out for a resource the dog considers valuable and the baby, of course, fails to notice signals of potential guarding displayed by the dog.

# EXISTING DOG – NEW ANIMAL/CAT

There are three fundamental points to remember when introducing a new animal to your house.

1. A major issue with introducing a new animal is that animals can be a bit more unpredictable and difficult to control than a baby! Chiefly, animals run when frightened and this is a prime factor in activating a dog's prey drive and the instinct to chase and, potentially, bite. Alternatively, if you're bringing in a fully grown cat rather than a kitten, the cat may not take kindly to an unknown dog and give the dog a real hiding. Not a great start. The environment must therefore be managed much more carefully than when introducing something that we can control, like a baby, and the introductions need to be much more structured.

2. Remember, unless you're Usain Bolt, your dog can move much faster than you. For this reason, create extra distance and security layers when introducing him to an animal that runs or something that might fight back. Give yourself some much-needed time to react if it all goes wrong.

3. You will need to take into account a number of factors when considering the level of risk involved in the introduction:

a. Firstly, your dog's history of previous encounters with other similar animals. If you're bringing in a new cat or chickens, is your dog already socialised with these animals or does he like to chase them? The introductions process is going to be much quicker and the level of risk much lower if your dog already has positive associations with the species of the new animal. I would be very careful introducing Frank to a cat since he's not really had very much to do with them. Chickens on the other hand are likely to be less of a problem. Whilst he's not been around them for a few years, he was raised with them and is also, by association, totally and utterly calm around pigeons, ducks, geese, etc.

b. Secondly, what is your level of control over your dog? Does he know how to sit, lie down, leave it, etc., especially in the face of distractions and when he is aroused?

c. Thirdly, you need to take into account the temperament of your dog. Is he an introvert and will just watch the new animal from a distance? Is he an extrovert and will want to go and explore, potentially frightening the new animal? Is he fearful or anxious? If so, this could cause over-reactivity.

Depending on the new animal AND your dog's proclivities and breed predispositions, risk management may involve the use of suitable barriers to avoid mishaps and ensure the safety of all, rather than just keeping the dog tethered on a lead.

# DOS

- Ensure the cat has a safe room that is inaccessible to the dog and contains everything necessary to meet the cat's needs, including water, litter tray, scratching post, etc.
- Ensure that communal spaces accessible to both the dog and cat have a number of height levels accessible only to your cat. If a cat is cornered or feels threatened, it will attack.
- Introduce the scent of the cat to the dog and vice versa for a few days before the visual introduction. You could do this by stroking or holding each animal in turn. Each will be able to smell the other on you. Alternatively, the animals could visit each other's rooms and check out the bedding and toys. Another way to scent swap could be to swap beds if the animals are of a similar size.
- Feed the animals at the same time but in separate rooms on either side of a closed door.
- Ensure initial meetings are short, in the garden or another large communal area and that the dog is secured on a lead. The cat can be left free. She is unlikely to get too close. This is again all about ensuring that the dog's arousal levels do not get so high that the thinking part of the brain is compromised and he becomes totally oblivious to any instructions from you.
- Present your dog with his top treat (cooked sausage? roast chicken?) throughout the duration of time he sees the cat. This will help him develop positive associations with the cat. This is classical conditioning at work. The dog is with the cat, and something great happens. So, the dog has a positive emotional response. What we don't want is for the dog to feel any unpleasantness when the cat is around. In that scenario, the dog would end up having a negative emotional response.
- Only allow unrestrained access after many sessions of the pair getting on well together. Even at this stage, you could leave a long lead on the dog so you can put a halt to the proceedings easily.

If you're of the ultra-nervous disposition or just not 100% certain of how your dog will react, you could get him to wear a muzzle on the first unrestrained meeting.

## DON'TS

- Rush the process. Only allow unsupervised meetings once you are absolutely certain the animals get on well at close quarters.
- Continue introductions if arousal levels get too high or there is any body language from either animal that suggests they are uncomfortable.
- Hold your dog or cat when making introductions. If they become stressed, you will be the first to get injured, due to redirected aggression.
- Confine either animal, e.g., in a crate, when making the introduction. This can be distressing for the confined pet.
- Make introductions at close quarters. The bigger the distance the better. Initially, try to put 20 feet or more between the animals, if you can manage it. Try to imagine your first ever introduction to a tarantula. I know I wouldn't want it thrust into my face. I'd like the handler and the tarantula to be many, many metres away, thank you very much.
- Add to any tension by getting excited yourself, shouting or being anxious. Try to take a chill pill before introductions.

# EXISTING DOG – NEW PUPPY

There are three fundamental points to remember here:

1. It's not a TV advert. People always expect the older dog to instantly fall in love with the puppy. Heck, it took me nearly a month to actually become besotted with my newborn son! Before that, he was just a newborn baby who I knew needed protecting and constant care.

Different dogs will react differently to a new puppy. Sure, some – and you often see videos of golden retrievers on social media – take an instant liking to the new puppy. Some, on the other hand, are very uncertain and choose to run away, especially when the puppy gives chase. Certainly, all my ridgebacks have fallen into the latter category. Ragnar was no different when initially introduced to Frank. Frank, being an extrovert, constantly wanted to play rough and tumble with

Ragnar. And why wouldn't he? That is precisely what he was used to with his littermates. Ragnar did what I thought he might – he ran away from Frank.

If all proceeds smoothly, the older dog will eventually allow the puppy to get closer, followed by looking at the puppy at close quarters and then, eventually, he'll entertain the puppy and put up with her licking his lips and ears and climbing all over him. In due course, your dog may even seek out the puppy and instigate play!

2. Separate the dogs regularly. Puppies are used to playing constantly with their siblings until it's food time or sleep time. That's unlikely to be the routine of your older dog. Sure, your dog will engage in play but the periods of play are shorter. And your dog won't enjoy being constantly bothered by an unruly pup.

3. The dogs should have separate sleeping areas. Dogs have three essential needs: physical, emotional and mental stimulation. Having a safe, comfortable place to sleep undisturbed is a crucial part of a dog's emotional needs.

## DOS BEFORE THE ARRIVAL

• Ask the breeder for a puppy-scented cloth for your dog. Let him live with this a week before the new puppy arrives. Take a blanket with your dog's scent and bring the puppy home swaddled in that.

• Tidy up any poo remains in the garden and ensure the existing dog's vaccinations are up to date and that he is generally well. Coprophagia is not uncommon in puppies. It's a habit they often grow out of, but not something you want to facilitate. Obviously, this clearing up of dog excrement continues to apply once the puppy has arrived

• Use crates, baby gates and pens to set up safe areas where either dog can be stationed and remain unbothered by the other. Let your existing dog get used to these items.

## DOS ON THE DAY OF ARRIVAL

• Ensure the dogs meet in a neutral place to avoid any territorial issues, maybe a garden belonging to a friend or neighbour. Preferably the garden will be substantial in size with a raised area where the older dog can escape to.

- Initially, hold the puppy and allow the older dog to sniff the puppy's rear. Do this several times and treat both dogs for each successful sniff. If you've already scent swapped, this should be easier for both dogs.
- Only if all is going well, release both, with the older dog initially being on the raised level of the garden. That way, he can instigate further investigation at his own pace.
- Only after they have become a little more comfortable in a neutral location, should you take them inside. Keep the pup in a crate or behind a baby gate.

## DOS IN THE WEEKS THAT FOLLOW

- Always supervise interactions for the first few weeks. Restrict play to short periods. Stop the interactions well before the pup starts to irritate the older dog with his constant play. Leave both dogs wanting more.
- Choose separate feeding areas to prevent the puppy running up to older dog's bowl and vice versa. This may appear cute, but I've found there is often a link between sharing feeding areas and development of resource guarding issues.
- Put away all dog toys or anything else that might prompt guarding to avoid potential conflict and future resource guarding problems.
- No telling off. If you do hear a growl, don't punish the growler; change the environment. Behaviour is a form of communication. We don't want to stop or discourage communication.
- If the puppy is being inappropriate or bothering the older dog, you can intervene. This is particularly the case when the older dog has already given the puppy a gentle warning.
- Follow the old dog's routine and establish a separate routine for the puppy.
- Spend quality time with both dogs separately, including play and training. Hard work, I know, but we want to keep the upheaval caused by a new puppy to a minimum.
- Always ensure there are plenty of opportunities for the older dog to escape the puppy and have somewhere peaceful to rest.

Generally, the older dog will, after a few weeks, start to relish the company of the puppy. Here are some photographs of Ragnar beginning to enjoy Frank's company.

## DON'TS

- Force interactions or rush the pace of bonds being forged. As we've discussed, go at the older dog's pace.
- Allow your dog to take things from the puppy. This may lead to resource guarding behaviours from the puppy as she matures.
- Favour one dog over the other – particularly allowing one to sit close to you but not the other.
- Allow both to crowd you during play. Ask each to sit whilst the other is petted. Teach them this early. As the dogs mature, this rushing up and wanting to be petted at the same time can be a trigger that starts off a fight.

# EXISTING CHILDREN – NEW DOG

To a large extent, the advice given under the 'new baby' section applies here. The danger here is that children and toddlers are mobile. Without supervision, young children can easily interact with the dog in a way that can create a negative emotional experience for the dog. This can lead to the dog becoming anxious and fearful around all children and result in unwanted behaviours such as growling, snapping or even biting.

With the above in mind, let's look at the dos and don'ts that will hopefully lead to a very happy relationship between the children and the new dog.

# DOS

- Teach your toddler/children that the dog is not a toy. The children can play with the dog when the dog wants to play with the children.
- Ensure any petting is supervised, and use baby gates to ensure your child can't get to the dog without your involvement. Depending on the age of the child, and until a very firm positive relationship has been formed, petting should be done with the back of the hand to the side of the dog's body, starting from the shoulder and going to the hindquarters.
- Ensure the child is sitting rather than standing when interacting with the dog. We do not want an accident where the child falls on or stands on the dog's paws. That is likely to cause negative associations with children for that dog.
- Ask the children to move at half their normal speed. Make it a challenging game of skill for the child. Children acting in an excited manner (probably incessantly!) makes the dog excited, and high arousal levels compromise the thinking part of the dog's brain. Furthermore, this also reinforces boisterous behaviour.
- Give the dog choice on when to interact with the children. If the dog goes away, let him go. If the dog stays, continue to let the children gently stroke him. As always, remember to keep initial interaction sessions short.
- Create positive associations. Invite your dog over when playing with your child and vice versa. Each time the child comes over when you are playing with the dog, you should treat the dog and then the child should offer a treat placed in his open palm. Each time the dog comes over, offer him a treat if he is calm or after he has offered you a behaviour that you have requested, e.g., down. The child may also offer a treat in his outstretched hand.
- Your dog should have access to a calm quiet undisturbed rest area/room. This will help meet his emotional needs.
- Take extra precautions if the new dog is a puppy. Interactions may need to be restricted to the puppy being behind a baby gate or on a harness – particularly when he hasn't yet learned about bite

inhibition. Interactions should take place when the puppy is in a calm mood, not at the 'witching hour' that seems to affect all puppies. During the witching hour (around 6 p.m.), puppies just don't listen to rhyme or reason due to their over-tired or over-aroused state.

• Take extra precautions if your dog is a rescue. It can take three months for a rescue dog to show his true colours. The dog may need to wear a muzzle until you are absolutely certain that his temperament and behaviour around young children is calm and trustworthy.

# DON'TS

• Allow the child to access the dog's treats, toys, food or water bowl. This can very quickly lead to resource guarding issues, especially if the child misses the warning signs that a dog is uncomfortable with someone approaching his toy, bed or food bowl.

• Allow children access to the dog whilst he is resting. Startling a dog can cause the dog to snap, and disturbing his sleep is unlikely to satisfy his emotional needs.

• Treat the dog as a toy. Being picked up against his will is, in due course, likely to cause him to react against it. Furthermore, there is a risk that the dog may be dropped, causing injury and psychological trauma. Remember, traumatic events are one of the main causes of dogs becoming fearful of similar events in the future.

• Allow a child to approach the dog unsupervised. You need to be on top of things to avoid children acting in a way that might upset the dog, and you need to be able to intervene at the first sign of the dog communicating that he is finding the encounter unpleasant.

• Persist in interaction sessions if the dog shows any signs of discomfort.

• Allow any hugging or kissing. I see a lot of this on social media – the photo might be cute, but the dog is often showing all the signs of being uncomfortable with the stranglehold hug! The fact of the matter is that whilst some don't mind being hugged, many dogs find this unpleasant as the child is encroaching on the dog's personal space. Any warning bite in such a situation is also likely to take place in the face area. Not ideal. If you're not sure which camp your dog falls into when it comes to hugs, I think the safest approach is to avoid hugging and kissing. Stroking the head can also be intimidating for many dogs. Far better to hold out a hand and, if the dog is willing, initially stroke him under his chin.

# A FEW THINGS TO KEEP IN MIND

First, to achieve long-lasting, positive relationships between animals, the dos and don'ts are designed not only to classically condition our dog, but also to operantly condition him. See more on this in Chapter 11.

**Operant conditioned behaviours** are voluntary behaviours. Performing the behaviour is a conscious act by the dog, voluntarily offered where there is a reward for him. In other words, there is a valuable outcome that can be achieved following the behaviour.

Here are some examples to illustrate operant conditioning. You say sit; the dog sits because he's learned there's a treat in it for him. The dog is a counter surfer and has learnt that when he does this, he is sometimes rewarded by finding something tasty. The dog barks at the postman, and the postman goes away (he was always going to go away); because the dog was rewarded by the postman going away, he gets a valuable outcome, which will encourage him to repeat his behaviour next time the postman visits.

In contrast, **classically conditioned behaviours** are not voluntary but reflexive in nature. They become an automatic reaction in the dog, created by the dog noticing that a particular event/condition precedes something good or something unpleasant. Therefore, the environment starts to affect the dog's biology or bodily conditions.

For example, you take out a lead; the dog does a happy dance. The lead is of no intrinsic value, but it precedes something good that's going to happen and leads to a positive emotional response. Rescue dogs often have trouble with men, and especially men in uniforms.

That's because it's often men (often in uniforms) that catch them. The dog comes to associate men with something unpleasant, which leads to a negative emotional response. This is classical conditioning.

Therefore, the dos and don'ts in this chapter are designed not only to classically condition a dog to have positive associations with new babies, new puppies, new cats and so on, but also to operantly condition the dog by rewarding him when he performs behaviours we like. This is because when behaviours we like are reinforced – for example, calmness around a baby – the dog becomes more likely to repeat those calm behaviours.

Secondly, as discussed in Chapter 6, it is crucial to bear in mind distance, duration of sessions and the intensity of the new introduction (distraction) when we are teaching our dog to behave calmly.

Finally, we must only use positive, reward-based training techniques and not punishment-based training methods. Punishment-based methods like telling the dog off or shouting at him are not going to do very much for our ultimate aim of conditioning the dog to learn that the baby, cat or puppy is something to look forward to.

# CHAPTER 11 –
# MODIFYING UNWANTED
# BEHAVIOURS – BASIC PRINCIPLES

There are several common behaviour modification principles and action plans that are effective in modifying unwanted behaviours and encouraging acceptable behaviours.

Dog trainers are usually consulted to help with behaviours that fall into one or more of the following three categories:

- **Behaviours that are to be expected due to the age or breed of the dog.** Behaviours that fall into this category could include, for example, puppies mouthing, jumping up, chewing the furniture or having toileting issues. In adolescent dogs, this could include barking, not listening, or exuberant behaviours. Older dogs might exhibit grumpy behaviours towards younger dogs and children and not comply with cues with the same alacrity that they once did.

With this category of behaviours, owners normally need simple guidance on the underlying reasons for the behaviours, followed by suggestions on how to effectively manage the environment to help the dog succeed, together with guidance on how best to teach their dog about which behaviours are unacceptable and which behaviours are required of them.

- **Behaviours that may be normal for the age/breed of the dog or are just beyond normal and are difficult to manage due to their intensity or frequency.** Behaviours in this category could include inappropriate urine marking, separation anxiety, excessive mounting, excessive barking, chasing cyclists or over-activity in response to a variety of stimuli in the environment. These types of behaviours are unlikely to be resolved by straightforward training or simple management of the environment, and are likely to require the implementation of specific behaviour modification strategies.

• **Behaviours that are extremely severe, intense and often described by clients as unusual, abnormal or dysfunctional.** These behaviours are commonly linked to mental health, pathological issues or emotional disorders. These behaviours include stereotypical behaviours (e.g., circling, light chasing, excessive grooming, etc.), established and ingrained bite history, debilitating anxiety, destructive behaviour and behaviours that often impact on the health and wellbeing of the dog, other people or other dogs. For these types of behaviours, in addition to behavioural strategies, medical intervention may be required to ease the underlying anxieties, fears and medical issues to put the dog in a state of mind to enable learning to take place.

We have already discussed the impact of various medical conditions on behaviour in Chapter 4. To ensure behaviours caused by medical conditions are ruled out as a potential cause for these behaviours or alternatively addressed, veterinarian involvement is prudent. This is particularly the case when a behavioural problem falls into the last two categories or there's a sudden change in behaviour. The vet may be able to link the behaviour exhibited to a medical condition afflicting the dog, and may be able to prescribe appropriate medication to provide relief from the underlying medical problem. Drugs might target endocrine problems, pain, bacterial infections, epilepsy disorder, or emotional anxieties and fears.

Not only can medical conditions or drugs that have already been prescribed for the dog affect his behaviour, so can dietary intolerances/sensitivities. Dietary sensitivity can cause a number of behavioural concerns. Aggression, anxiety and compulsive behaviours have all been associated with, and recognised as, arising from dietary sensitivities. Without a thorough investigation by the veterinarian to check for dietary intolerances that might be causing the problem, the behaviour might appear somewhat random and unpredictable.

In addition to prescribed medication, a veterinarian should also be able to discuss complementary and more natural remedies. These complementary therapies could include one or more of the following: homeopathy, Bach flower remedies, acupuncture, Tellington TTouch®, the Bowen technique, reiki and synthetic dog-appeasing pheromones. There's not an awful amount of scientific research on the effectiveness of these complementary therapies (other than the pheromones), but there is a growing body of anecdotal evidence as to their effectiveness.

# BEHAVIOUR MODIFICATION PRINCIPLES

In this chapter, we'll have a look at some of the behaviour modification principles that you're likely to come across and can use to deal with a whole host of behavioural problems. Understand these principles, and you'll soon be on the way to solving any unwanted behaviour your dog might exhibit.

## OPERANT CONDITIONING

In a nutshell, operant conditioning is all about the science of dogs repeating voluntary behaviours for which there is a positive or negative reinforcement and not repeating behaviours for which there is no reinforcement or for which there is a positive or negative unpleasant consequence (called 'punishment').

Positive reinforcement/rewards involve giving something (e.g., a food treat) to your dog when he does something you like and want more of. Negative reinforcement/rewards instead involve taking something unpleasant away as soon as the dog does what you want. This could be, for example, taking away the hand pressure forcing the dog to sit as soon as he does sit.

Positive punishment/unpleasantness might include telling the dog off for a behaviour you don't like. Negative punishment/unpleasantness might include taking away something pleasant until you do get the behaviour you want. This could be removing yourself from the room if your dog is being boisterous, and re-entering the room only when he calms down.

We touched on operant conditioning in previous chapters, and I suggested that you should train your dog using positive reinforcement/rewards. You should avoid using the negative reinforcement/rewards discussed above. Equally, you should avoid punishments/unpleasant consequences, whether they be positive or negative. While punishment-based strategies can sometimes work, there is often fallout and other undesired behaviours can set in as a result.

# CLASSICAL CONDITIONING

Unlike operant conditioned behaviours, classically conditioned behaviours are not voluntary and are not conscious acts by the dog. Instead, they are reflexive in nature and the dog has no control over them. These are things such as salivation or feeling anxious or feeling good.

Because of conditioning, the environment affects the dog's biology or bodily conditions. It's all about dogs noticing that something in the environment is an indicator that something good, or something unpleasant, will happen.

Take out a lead, dog does a happy dance. The lead is of no intrinsic value but it predicts something good is going to happen. A positive emotional response.

On the other hand, rescue dogs often have trouble with men. That's because it's often men that catch them. The dog comes to associate men with something unpleasant. A negative emotional response.

# DESENSITISATION

This is used to work with dogs that have developed a fear of something. This could be other dogs, people, a specific group of people such as children or men, specific noises, vehicles, skateboards. The list is endless. My dog, Ragnar, once developed a fear of a particular radiator in the house. And this was after he had slept next to the radiator for over two years! Mind you, he is a Rhodesian ridgeback – the breed really should be renamed to Rhodesian wussback!

How do these fears arise? Well, we discussed this in Chapter 4. But to recap, it could be due to a lack of socialisation, some traumatic experience, genetic issues, medical conditions affecting the brain or even a stressful perinatal environment. Of course, it could just be the most minor of movements or sounds experienced by a dog during his particularly sensitive fear periods.

The purpose of desensitisation is to gradually accustom a dog to the presence of a specific fearful stimulus in order to extinguish the fear response. By way of example: if you're scared of wasps (maybe you were stung once), you may respond to the sight of a wasp by flailing your arms about, screaming your head off and then running around like a headless chicken. This is exactly what my younger sister does! Some dogs carry out similar behaviours when they see something that frightens them. Your dog sees another dog and he starts to bark, pull on the lead, lunge, growl or maybe even cower and shake with fear. Fear responses only arise when a fearful stimulus leaves the dog's **'safe zone'** and enters his **'worry zone'**.

Think of the worry zone as a circle around the dog. Anything the dog fears that is in the circle will bother him. The radius of the circle is different for each dog. Anything he fears in the safe zone (outside the worry zone) doesn't bother him and he is unlikely to react to it.

The gold standard of successfully desensitising a dog to fearful visual stimuli, e.g., children (or my sister of wasps for that matter), requires the adherence to two rules. First, ensure that you always work with the fearful stimuli outside the dog's worry zone and, therefore, in his safe zone. Secondly, the exposure should increase in challenge, starting with the least difficult. We can satisfy the second aspect of desensitisation by practising bursts of brief exposure (e.g., five seconds) at long distances for short training sessions (e.g., two minutes) with around a 30 second break between each exposure. Gradually, and at the dog's pace, you can then build up to longer exposures (e.g., a minute), shorter distances (but always outside the worry zone) and longer sessions (e.g., ten minutes) – again with 30 second breaks between exposures to help the dog to reset.

It could be that your dog is worried about a particular noise e.g., fireworks. Well, bearing in mind the above two aspects of desensitisation, exposure would initially involve playing the sound of fireworks at a low enough volume that it does not bother your dog at all. Eventually the volume can be increased at a pace that suits the dog. Worry zones in terms of noise relate to the volume level of the sound.

If the two rules of desensitisation are followed, it means that the 'size' of the fearful stimulus is minimised to such a level that it isn't frightening and, therefore, doesn't evoke the existing fear and the consequent response. Over time, the dog's worry zone will decrease and the original fear response will be extinguished. However, whilst the response may become extinct and the dog may come to feel neutral and unfazed by the once fearful stimulus, it does not necessarily mean that he will come to actually like the stimulus – e.g., children jumping up and down near him. The fear response may still remain, and it may just be that the worry zone has shrunk to such an extent that you don't notice the fear response as the stimulus is always in the dog's safe zone. To actually change the dog's emotions so he comes to see the fearful stimulus as positive rather than negative, we should utilise the principle of counterconditioning.

# COUNTERCONDITIONING

Counterconditioning is used to change the dog's emotional mindset about a particular stimulus. For example, if the dog becomes fearful or anxious at the sight of an approaching man and reacts accordingly by barking and lunging or cowering, the aim of counterconditioning is to help the dog regard approaching men as something pleasant. This, in turn, also changes his response to become calm and friendly rather than reactive.

Counterconditioning is achieved by constantly and repeatedly pairing a stimulus the dog considers negative and unpleasant with something that is emotionally pleasant. Normally we use primary reinforcers – those rewards that are linked to biological drives, like food or sex. Since we can't turn to sex, best to use the dog's other absolute favourite: food! We can sometimes use conditioned reinforcers, such as a game that your dog loves the most and to which he is addicted. However, remember that a game will only work if the dog has already associated it with something pleasant.

This pairing is continued until the dog forms a positive association with the negative stimulus. This makes the dog like the stimulus. Before long, he will be happy to see the hitherto negative stimulus as he comes to predict that whenever he sees the stimulus, it brings about good things (such as his favourite cooked sausage or roast chicken).

An experiment involving a three-year-old child called Peter, in 1924 by Mary Cover Jones, showed counterconditioning in humans at work. The child had a fear of rabbits. He was given milk and crackers each time a rabbit was presented outside his worry zone. The worry zone decreased and the rabbit was gradually moved closer. Gradually, the child was able to pet the rabbit with one hand whilst eating a cracker with the other. Of course, hygiene, health and safety considerations might prevent this experiment from taking place today.

Counterconditioning is generally undertaken hand-in-hand with desensitisation. It is difficult for a dog to eat his favourite food if the stimulus is already in his worry zone.

A good way to implement counterconditioning is to first present the fearful stimulus to the dog outside his worry zone. Let's say the thing that causes your dog concern is men. As soon as the dog sees the man, the food should be presented. Importantly, as soon as the man disappears, the food treats cease. It is important for the dog to understand that only the presence of the fearful stimulus predicts something good is going to occur each time (food treats). It is equally important for the dog to understand that once the fearful stimulus is no longer there, neither is the food stuff.

# EXTINCTION

We have touched on this principle before; it involves the ending of a behaviour by removing all the reinforcement previously fuelling it. Simply ignoring behaviours which were previously reinforced, is not a method of which I am overly fond. This is partly because for the dog, offering you the behaviour is a form of communication in which you previously participated and encouraged. To now simply ignore the behaviour is unfair and could lead to frustration and/or distress for the dog. The second problem with extinguishing behaviours in this way is that it can cause extinction bursts. This means the dog will actually intensify the behaviour when he senses that it isn't working and feels distressed about you ignoring him. In addition, even though the behaviour might become extinct, sometimes it can reappear when you're least expecting it – this is known as spontaneous recovery.

So, how best to remove behaviours that you previously rewarded, such as jumping up at you? The best way to deal with this is not just to ignore the behaviour, but to immediately reward the alternate behaviour your dog does offer and which you want – such as, in this instance, having all four paws on the floor. This is much kinder and avoids the potential distress caused by simply ignoring your dog for jumping up. This method is also good for helping clarify in your dog's mind which behaviours aren't rewarded (and therefore not worthy of repeating) and which behaviours are rewarded – and therefore worthy of repeating!

# RESPONSE SUBSTITUTION

Response substitution helps the dog replace an undesirable response, such as barking or lunging, with a more desirable one, such as looking at you – always through positive reinforcement. The desirable behaviour can either be requested or it might just be offered by the dog. So, you might teach the dog that when he sees another dog, he should look at you, or sit, or play ball with you, rather than eyeball or growl at the other dog. Likewise, if the postman knocks on the door, you might ask your dog to go to his bed or to another room rather than running and barking at the door. These more desirable behaviours are usually incompatible with the undesirable behaviour. Your dog can't rush the door if he's been asked to lie on his bed. Your dog can't eyeball another dog if he's focusing on you and a ball. This is what trainers call differential reinforcement of incompatible behaviours (DRI).

Alternatively, you might request, or your dog might carry out of his own accord, a behaviour that is an acceptable alternative to (rather than incompatible with) the undesirable behaviour. That alternative behaviour might simply be looking at something else or any calm behaviour. If you were to reward this alternative behaviour, it would be known as differential reinforcement of alternative behaviours (DRA).

Whether we reward incompatible behaviours or alternative behaviours, it teaches the dog to repeat such desirable behaviours rather than the undesirable behaviour (which should not be rewarded).

# HABITUATION

Habituation is all about presenting stimuli in a sympathetic way so that there is a gradual lessening of a response to the stimulus. Habituation occurs when a stimulus is repeatedly presented to the dog. The dog comes to learn that the stimulus does not signal anything important and is simply part of the environment. Hoovers, washing machines, lawnmowers, cars, etc., all fall into the sort of items to which you would want to habituate your dog.

Habituation is similar to desensitisation. The difference is that habituation is used when the dog has not already become fearful of a stimulus. However, if the hoover or whatever else is not introduced in a positive way, it is all too clear to see how a dog may become conditioned to fear it. At that stage, the principle of desensitisation would be used to remove the fear response.

## MEDICAL INTERVENTION

In conjunction with the use of behaviour modification strategies, veterinarian involvement is often necessary to help modify problem behaviours, because behaviours are often linked to medical issues. Here are some common cases where a prompt referral to a vet should be made:

- Changes in appetite/weight/activity levels.
- Skin or ear issues. The dog may be shaking his head more than normal or you might detect a bad odour from the ears. With skin issues, you may see more frequent itching.
- A sudden change in behaviour.
- The dog is uncomfortable during handling or petting.
- The dog has recently been prescribed new medication and his behaviour has changed.
- Recent injuries.

# CHAPTER 12 – RESOLVING COMMON BEHAVIOURAL PROBLEMS

Before assessing the best strategies and action plans to change any given unwanted behaviour, we need to clarify three things.

First, assess the motivation and function of the particular problem behaviour. For example, if your dog is barking incessantly, is it because he is stressed and sounding the alarm, or does he want to elicit play, or is it because he suffers from separation anxiety and wants to be near you? As another example, if your dog is destructively chewing furniture, is it due to boredom, or teething, or lack of exercise, or stress caused by things in the environment?

Secondly, consider and be clear about everything that takes place in the environment before the unwanted behaviour takes place (we call these antecedents) and all the things that happen in the environment after the behaviour happens (we call these consequences).

Finally, it is important to understand the relevant breed-specific, environmental and, potentially, medical causes of the behaviours. If you consult a behaviourist, he will ask standard questions relating to the above and also regarding diet, training history and exercise regime. This gives behaviourists an indication of your dog's personality and capabilities.

If your dog is showing any agonistic behaviours, expect any consultant to query the following details at the very least:

- Date of the first incident.
- Whether multiple incidents have taken place – has the behaviour been regularly practised?

- Whether anything has recently changed in the dog's world – e.g., diet change or change of house.
- Whether the owners understand dog body language and warning signals prior to a biting incident.
- The owner's reaction to the behaviour. Sometimes, the owner's subsequent behaviour can make the behaviour worse, especially if aversives have been used, such as shouting, telling the dog off, yanking the lead, or hitting the dog.
- The dog's reaction after the incident.
- The severity of any injuries caused by biting. If a number of bites have caused serious injury, euthanisation may need to be considered as an option. It should be borne in mind that even if a bite was not severe on one occasion, it does not mean that it won't be more severe next time. If the behaviour has got worse over time, the consultant will need to understand the reasons for this.

In the pages that follow, I'll discuss a number of dog behaviours that commonly cause owners and the dog difficulties. We'll look at why these behavioural problems might arise in the first instance and strategies you could use to change those behaviours to something more acceptable. All the strategies and action plans set out have been used on real life cases and have been effective, and they all aim to make the dog want to do things through positive reinforcement methods rather than through force and fear.

I should also mention a caveat when it comes to modifying ingrained undesirable dog behaviours. This book provides great guidance on what's going on in your dog's mind, as well as the principles and strategies used in modifying behaviour. But all dogs are different. This is not only because of their breed characteristics, but also because they are all very individual in how they react to stimuli and behaviour modification strategies. Given this, there is considerable merit in using the services of behaviourist to assess those individual characteristics and, importantly, to demonstrate the application of the action plans set out in the following pages.

# SEPARATION ANXIETY

Owners often complain that when they go to another room, their dog stands near the door, continuously barking and whining, or just won't settle. When the owner leaves the home, dogs can display numerous behaviours including barking incessantly, salivating, whining, destruction of doors or sofas, pacing, etc. These behaviours are born out of distress at the owner leaving the dog's presence. When dogs display any of these behaviours, people commonly refer to the dog as suffering from separation anxiety or separation-related disorders. I consider true separation anxiety a medical emergency.

Separation anxiety can be caused by a number of environmental factors:

• The dog has become accustomed to his owner's constant presence and has difficulty being alone.

• The dog's response to the owner's absence can become learned through success in being reunited with the owner whenever he whines or barks when left alone.

• An owner's own stressful life can be picked up by the dog, causing him stress and leading to separation anxiety.

• Major changes in the dog's home life can cause emotional distress for the dog and lead to separation anxiety.

In assessing whether your dog is suffering from separation anxiety, remember that other factors can cause dogs to become distressed. Such factors must be ruled out. For example, if noises in the environment are causing him distress and setting him off, eliminate or habituate him to these first or have white noise in the background to mask them.

## WHAT'S GOING ON IN THE DOG'S MIND?

Most dogs feel emotionally calm, relaxed and contented when they are with their owner, due to the release of neuropeptides including endogenous opioids, oxytocin and prolactin.

When owners leave, certain behaviours such as barking are indicative of distress and the arousal of the panic/grief system. Once so aroused, the neuropeptides glutamate and corticotrophin-releasing factor (CRF) are at elevated levels and the stress response, involving the release of stress hormones including cortisol, is set into motion.

The dog's motivation is, therefore, to deactivate the distressing panic/grief system and the accompanying chemicals. As such, the motivation is linked to dopamine systems. The function of the whining is to reduce distance and reunite with the owner. The reinforcement of the behaviour comes from the endogenous opioids, prolactin and oxytocin released once the dog is reunited with the owner.

Furthermore, due to the internal neurochemical reinforcement in the form of dopamine, the dog learns through positive reinforcement that his behaviour works to keep the owner by his side. Consequently, the dog is likely to continue, and escalate, his distress vocalisations.

# HOW TO RESOLVE SEPARATION ANXIETY

In resolving separation anxiety, I would advocate implementation of all the general and specific steps set out below.

## GENERAL ADVICE

- To help ensure the effectiveness of the protocols below, make a habit of playing with your dog and ensure you meet the dog's essential needs, including mental stimulation to help his mood. Specifically, allow your dog to have additional exercise and socialisation through at least a couple of off-lead walks per day.
- Always have someone to care for your dog when you need to leave the home until his separation anxiety related behaviour has been resolved.
- Get a veterinarian check-up and ask for prescription medication in case you need to leave your dog to go out in an emergency. The vet may prescribe benzodiazepine for this purpose and/or recommend the use of dog-appeasing pheromones.
- Sometimes, conditioning your dog to settle in his crate and see it as his safe place can help. The dog then doesn't have to worry about checking your whereabouts through the curtains or at the door. This certainly worked for one of my clients. The dog used to be crated as a pup, but in later life, the crate was removed. The dog developed separation-related disorders and would constantly

whine whenever the owners left the room or the home. As soon as she was re-crated, cameras showed that she miraculously settled after a couple of minutes of the owners leaving the home.

- Choose a visual or auditory signal that will enable your dog to predict that whenever the signal is present, he will be ignored. For example, you could switch a light or radio on. Alternatively, you could draw the curtains. This is discussed further in the specific steps below.
- If your dog is used to constantly being with you, regularly send him away or cut out sofa time altogether (you can always go and stroke him on his bed).
- Ask your dog to go to his crate/bed in a separate room from time to time.
- Get yourself a camera so you can spy on him and see what he does in your absence, particularly his body language.

## SPECIFIC STEPS

This modification plan involves three separate stages.

**Stage 1** – Over a period of 14 days, teach your dog, through positive reinforcement, to stay in a chosen location (e.g., bed) in a relaxed and unaroused state for five minutes. The aim is for your dog to remain in a relaxed state whilst you go about your business. This exercise should increase in degrees of difficulty involving distance, distraction and duration, as discussed in Chapter 6.

- Initially ask your dog to sit for five seconds, then take a couple of steps away. You could then increase the difficulty for your dog, perhaps by gently waving your hands or hopping on the spot for a few seconds. You could then open and close a drawer and then return and praise your dog for remaining in a calm state.
- Then progress to stepping further away, for 15 seconds, touching the door handle, opening and closing the door, sitting on a chair, or jogging before rewarding calmness and a neutral state. Using this method of gradually increasing the challenge for your dog to remain calm will help you more easily identify the steps with which your dog is struggling.
- If your dog gets up, you are moving too fast. Either wait for him to sit/lie down or prompt him to sit/lie down and then restart with one second of calm and then two seconds.

- The increases in duration should be done gradually by alternating between long and short periods of duration. So, you could ask him to stay on his bed for 10 seconds before praising, then 30 seconds, then 15 seconds, then 1 minute, then 20 seconds, then 45 seconds and so on.

- You should use treats that your dog finds extremely reinforcing and that will motivate him to listen to you. Be generous. I find cooked sausage or roast chicken does the trick.

- As your dog manages to remain calm, the level of challenge should be increased. Require him to remain calm whilst you leave his sight briefly, knock on the door, sing, or have an imaginary conversation, and then return to praise your dog's calm state using intermittent reinforcement on a variable interval schedule.

- Relaxation exercises should be done in ten-minute sessions, three times per day. Each session should comprise three two-minute sessions with breaks in between to avoid pushing the dog past his limit and thereby inducing anxiety. This can be gradually built up to 15–20 minutes twice per day.

This stage will not only help your dog stay in a relaxed position, but also make him stop constantly following you everywhere you go without having to confine him to the crate. Try to achieve a target of your dog being able to stay in a relaxed state for around five minutes after two weeks of training.

**Stage 2** – Dogs can become slightly anxious/unsettled prior to owners leaving the home. This stage is designed to desensitise your dog to the cues that signal your departure and avoids him becoming stressed before you have even left.

Work out the cues that signal your departure and stress your dog out before you leave the house. Walking towards the front door? Picking up the door keys? Putting your coat on? These are all typical cues. Repeat the behaviours without actually leaving the house to help acclimatise your dog to them. Coats should be put on and taken off, keys should be picked up and then put down. Walk towards the door, open it, and close it again. Do this until the cues that set your dog off, no longer bother him, and he can stay relaxed while they're happening.

At each stage of this process, calm behaviour by your dog should be rewarded.

**Stage 3** – This stage, carried out over a period of four weeks, aims to desensitise and counter-condition your dog, and gradually teaches him not only to be relaxed when left alone for increasing increments of time, but find it a positive and rewarding experience rather than a stressful one.

Once you've completed the first two stages and ensured that the environment is conducive to your dog remaining calm and not becoming agitated, **Stage 3(a)** training starts with:

- Teaching your dog that when a certain signal is displayed, he will be ignored – I use 'Alexa, play Radio 4', which has the added benefit of masking any external environmental noises that might creep into the property and those awesomely powerful dog ears.

- Ignore the dog for 30 seconds, then take away the signal – I use 'Alexa, radio off'. That now signals to the dog that he will no longer be ignored. You should now interact with him. You could ask him to come to you for a stroke.

- Do this in small increments of time and only increase the time if your dog remains relaxed, i.e., loose body, relaxed mouth, ears soft and hanging.

- Build up to ignoring your dog for three to five minutes.

- There is no need to provide a chew when building up time.

Once you can ignore your dog for three to five minutes without him displaying any behaviour other than remaining relaxed, progress to **Stage 3(b)**:

- Initially touch, and then open and close the door whilst your dog remains calm on his bed.

- You can then progress to stepping outside the doorway and then returning before shutting the door. Eventually, your dog should sit and stay relaxed whilst you close the door behind you. Start with leaving for five seconds before re-entering, removing the signal and interacting with/praising your dog in a calm manner.

- Gradually increase the time spent outside in increments of a few seconds or so at a time.

- When ignoring the dog during deployment of the signal, do not extend the time spent ignoring him in a linear fashion. Instead, use a zig-zag time interval, e.g., 10s, 20s, 10s, 30s,10s, 20s, 30s, 20s, 30s, 10s, 60s. Over the coming weeks, increase the time to two minutes, then five, then ten.

- Allow mini breaks between absences to allow your dog to reset.

- The goal is for your dog to remain calm for thirty minutes or so, after which he should be able to withstand longer periods of separation. The reward schedule is as for Stage 1.
- Always make the longest absence the final absence for the session.

# MEDICAL INTERVENTION?

Often, separation anxiety is so intense that medical intervention will be appropriate. A veterinarian's advice is needed here on the potential benefits of specific medications.

Medications to help separation-related issues are best served with a dish of behavioural modification plans. Once the dog becomes desensitised to your absence for increased increments of time, the need for, and benefits (with some side effects) of medication can be reviewed.

I'll set out the brief details of some of the medications that your veterinarian may recommend, but ultimately, it is the veterinarian who'll advise you on this matter.

Your veterinarian might suggest serotonergic agents, including clomipramine and fluoxetine. There is evidence that a dose (1 to < 2 mg/kg, every 12 hours) of clomipramine for two to three months accompanied by behaviour modification therapy will help most dogs improve at least three times faster for the signs of destruction, defecation and urination, but not vocalisations. Mild and transient vomiting proved to be a side effect for some dogs. Other research suggests that this dose does in fact also reduce whining, whilst increasing the dose to 2mg/kg every 12 hours increases the time dogs are passive for AND reduces barking and whining.

Clomipramine is designed to increase levels of serotonin and norepinephrine in the body, which have a calming influence. So far as fluoxetine is concerned, there is evidence that even in the absence of a behaviour modification plan, fluoxetine reduces separation related behaviours, but it can take several weeks to take effect (just like clomipramine). Common side effects can include vomiting and diarrhoea.

Combining medications can also be beneficial. Evidence suggests that administering clonidine with clomipramine may further improve anxiety-related behaviour, and combining fluoxetine with clorazepate dipotassium may reduce signs of anxiety in non-aggressive dogs.

In addition, medications for helping behaviour modification for separation anxiety include benzodiazepines (BZs), which enhance the effect of GABA, thereby slowing down the activity of the fear and other affective systems. BZs include diazepam (Valium) and alprazolam (Xanax)

BZs have proved useful in some cases in combination with medications that influence serotonin metabolism, such as selective serotonin reuptake inhibitors (SSRIs) e.g., fluoxetine, and tricyclic antidepressants (TCAs), e.g., clomipramine, especially if the dog has phobias or experiences panic attacks.

BZs tend to be given one to two hours before an anxiety-inducing event such as fireworks and are for short-term use as opposed to fluoxetine and clomipramine, which are given on a longer-term basis and take several weeks to take effect.

Synthetic dog-appeasing pheromones can also be helpful in reducing anxiety and, therefore, anxiety-related behaviours. One study suggests that use of dog-appeasing pheromones (DAP) reduced certain separation anxiety behaviours in 83% of dogs as opposed to 73% of dogs on clomipramine. Another study suggests that DAP was more effective than clomipramine for reducing destructive behaviours, but that clomipramine was more effective than DAP regarding house-soiling.

It is worth bearing in mind that all medications have side effects and some can aggravate other issues, and that medications with a sedative effect involve a risk of dependency. The side effects drugs could have on other behavioural aspects must therefore be borne in mind when considering action plans for separation-related behaviours. Indeed, if any drug has a muscle-relaxant quality, the dog may experience flooding of stimuli, which, in the case of an anxious dog, may make his behaviour worse. Side effects of some drugs include increased aggression. If so, this will need to be even more carefully monitored if the dog is already predisposed to aggressive behaviours.

Blood and urine analysis is advised before medication use and during it at regular intervals to ensure internal organs are functioning normally. Furthermore, stopping medication should be a gradual process rather than an abrupt one. This is to avoid and monitor fluctuations in behaviours based on use of medication and any dependency-related behaviours that may have resulted from the medication.

# AGGRESSION TOWARDS PEOPLE

Several factors can cause aggression towards people. Some of these factors were discussed in Chapter 4. Invariably, dog aggression towards people, whether in the home or in public, is caused by lack of early socialisation or some historical trauma – which could be something as simple as tripping over the puppy and accidentally hurting it. Early socialisation (between 5 – 12 weeks and ongoing) with people outside the human family is vital to avoid this.

Dog aggression towards people may stem from nervousness and anxiety, which are often linked to insecurity and fear. Fear can manifest itself in a few ways. As we saw in Chapter 1, a fearful dog might cower and hide. However, barking, lunging and growling are also typical responses to fear. If these behaviours are unheeded, ultimately the only response left is to progress to biting.

Fear and anxiety can sometimes be due to medical issues. A veterinarian check, therefore, may be useful to ensure everything is normal, e.g., with thyroid function, especially if the aggression has happened suddenly and there isn't a pattern of previous learned aggressive behaviours.

If your dog has already bitten, nearly bitten or you suspect he could bite, acclimatising him to wearing a muzzle may be prudent, at least until the behaviour has been modified.

Many owners deal with their dog's aggression towards other people by avoiding people. If someone comes to the house, they might simply isolate the dog in another room. Alternatively, they may simply stop having people round. These 'solutions' are not necessarily the best way forward because the dog never gets the opportunity to learn to feel comfortable around people. And so, the reasons behind the aggressive behaviour remain unresolved.

## WHAT'S GOING ON IN THE DOG'S MIND?

When aggression towards people is caused by fear and anxiety, the motivation behind the barking and lunging is to gain safety. The function of the behaviour is generally to create distance between the dog and the stressor. Sometimes, the dog becomes so stressed and frustrated that nothing but a bite will do to release that stress. In those circumstances, the function of the behaviour will be to reduce the distance between the dog and the object of its stress and frustration.

The reinforcement for the behaviour is the relief felt once the distance has been created, either by the owner moving their dog away or the member of public moving away. It is this relief and the consequential release of endogenous opioids that is predicted by a neurotransmitter called dopamine. However, over time and repeated successes in achieving their motivation and function, dogs become less and less fearful. The behaviour, instead, becomes the dog's go-to position.

# HOW TO CHANGE THE AGGRESSIVE BEHAVIOUR

## GENERAL ADVICE

- In public, keep your dog on a lead and at a safe distance from the source of his fears. In other words, keep his fears outside his worry zone. The size of this is something that you will need to assess. It could be 10 feet, 20 feet or 100 feet.
- In public, calmly increase the distance if your dog barks at a stranger. You've obviously allowed someone to enter your dog's worry zone. If possible, simply turn and walk the other way. Next time, remember to use the eyes in the back of your head. Or, if you're Spider-Man, keep your Spidey senses switched on.
- Be matter-of-fact and confident. If your dog becomes anxious, you should let the dog see that you are not at all bothered by the source of his anxiety to the point of ignoring it.

- At all times, you should remain calm. Avoid shouting, raising your voice, speaking sharply, dragging your dog away or sharply tugging on his lead; these actions will heighten your dog's reaction when he is already highly aroused.
- Reward your dog when he is calm around strangers. The idea is that your dog should be rewarded for any behaviour that is alternative to, or incompatible with, aggressive behaviours.

## SPECIFIC ACTIONS FOR NERVOUSNESS AND AGGRESSION TOWARDS MEMBERS OF THE PUBLIC

- If your dog's aggression towards strangers is particularly intense and there is any risk that he might inflict a bite, it would be prudent to acclimatise him to wearing a muzzle in public.
- An appropriately marked jacket could be worn by your dog to notify others that he is of a nervous disposition. These jackets are often brightly coloured.
- If you sense any member of the public thinking of imposing on your dog, you should politely but firmly ask them to back off. These well-meaning people are exactly the sort that will make the matter much worse and normally know much less about dogs and their behaviours than they think. Avoid them like Covid-19 and all its variants.
- If you are walking your dog on a lead and you are confronted by an unexpected stranger drifting into your dog's worry zone, *calmly* move to a distance at which the stranger is in your dog's safe zone. Your dog will then be comfortable.
- Always practise strategies with the member of the public outside your dog's worry zone and in his safe zone.
- Let your dog see the source of his fear in his safe zone (sometimes called below threshold), where he is calm and shows no nervous behaviour. When he looks at the stranger, mark that behaviour by telling him 'Good boy' or 'yes' and give him a treat. Practise, practise, practise.

In due course, you won't even have to mark the behaviour. Your dog will see a person and, expecting a treat, look at you. So, treat him. This is exactly what we want. When he sees a person, he looks at you rather than barking or lunging. In this way, your dog will learn that strangers are the environmental cue that predict that good things (his favourite treat) will happen. At the same time, your dog is also learning the alternative behaviour that you do want – looking at you – since that is being rewarded. Soon, and after much repetition, the alternative, rewarded behaviour becomes the default, rather than the previously aggressive behaviour.

- **DO NOT show or give the treat to your dog before he has seen the stranger.** This risks the dog coming to regard the treat as something that predicts the stranger and, ergo, something unpleasant.
- Remember to use your Spidey sense to anticipate any fear by keeping the public in your dog's safe zone.
- Once strangers can pass by without your dog being affected, you may wish to progress to the next level and engage the stranger in a conversation.
- Once people can engage in a conversation without your dog being affected in a negative way, a further step to counterconditioning may be for him to accept a treat from strangers. But keep in mind the three Ds: distance, distraction, duration. When you increase the challenge and difficulty for your dog in one of these areas, you must decrease the challenge in another.
- Once the stranger has passed, treats must stop. We want your dog to understand that good things happen only when people are there.
- In due course, these strategies should classically condition your dog to look forward to receiving a treat or enjoy being petted by a stranger. But all dogs are different. If your dog has had very poor socialisation or has already bitten, this goal may take some time to achieve, and in some cases may never be fully realised. Nevertheless, dogs learn from accumulated experiences. It is important to ensure that each experience accumulated is a positive one. Every opportunity needs to be taken to put the above strategies in place. **A muzzle is advised for severe aggression cases, particularly where a dog has already bitten.** This simple precaution will not only put your mind at rest, but will also provide reassurance for members of the public.

In passing, I should say that it is perfectly normal for dogs to want maintain some distance from people that are not part of their social group. This can be observed in the behaviour of street dogs and feral dogs, which get the chance to exhibit many natural behaviours rather than be overly controlled by owners. These dogs, whilst they like to live around people, prefer to keep a little distance from them. Consequently, you should not feel any pressure from anyone to modify your dog's behaviour beyond him being able to feel comfortable with members of the public who do not encroach on his personal space.

## SPECIFIC ACTIONS FOR AGGRESSION TOWARDS VISITORS

- You can secure your dog to his bed ten minutes before the arrival of a guest using a hook and lead method, keeping him at a comfortable distance from where the guests will sit, but in full view. This part of the action plan requires you to have taught your dog to relax in his bed whilst you go about your business, rather than him following you everywhere. It also requires the dog to be totally comfortable being secured on a lead without visitors.

- You should advise guests to totally ignore the dog (no touching, no talking, and no eye contact). Of course, the general public sucks at ignoring a dog. The best they'll do is go completely still, stop breathing, clench their teeth and so on. What do dogs make of this? Well, it makes them even more uncomfortable as these actions are extremely alien to the dog and can make him wary and anxious. The idea of ignoring the dog is to just try and act as normally as possible, as if the dog doesn't exist.

- Guests should sit as far as possible from your dog. If possible, this should be a distance that evokes no nervousness or fear. The distance can be slowly reduced during future visits, subject to your dog being totally calm during previous encounters.

- Visitors should speak in calm tones, and move slowly and fluidly.

- The layout of your house may not permit visitors to sit at a distance that is totally comfortable for your dog. In these circumstances, all nervous body language or growling exhibited by the dog should be ignored.

- Any calm behaviour/non-nervous behaviour should be rewarded with a treat by you. Alternatively, if you feel more comfortable, you can proceed as suggested under the section dealing with members of the public. To repeat, as soon as your dog looks at the guest, and before he can bark, mark that behaviour and give him a treat. In due course, your dog will look at the guest and, expecting a treat, look at you rather than barking at the guest. Over time, you can reduce the amount of treats and extend the time between them.

- If your dog becomes comfortable with the visitor's presence, the visitor may gently toss a treat to him whilst he is still secured.
- The visitor should also calmly stand up and sit down again. This can progress to slowly moving about the house. Non-reactive behaviour in response to this should be rewarded by you and the visitor. The dog needs to get used to a visitor moving about.
- If your dog does not take treats from the visitor, go back a step and ignore him again; he is not ready and you are moving too fast. Dogs do not take food treats when they are afraid or nervous.
- In due course, your dog may accept a gentle and slow stroke of his side, hindquarters, chest or under his chin from the visitor. However, progression to this level of proximity is not at all necessary. For many owners, it is quite acceptable and the aim may be for the dog to simply be comfortable with visitors rather than displaying aggression. In any event, the visitor should avoid stroking the top of your dog's head. This is frightening for nervous dogs.
- Depending on the severity of the aggression towards the guest, many weeks or months down the line, and once your dog has remained incident free for a whole month, he should be muzzled. Once muzzled, after about ten minutes of being secured to his bed area, you should unhook him whilst still asking him to stay on his bed. There should be no reaction at this stage. Calmness should be lavishly praised by you.
- Should your dog decide to go near the visitor, the visitor can calmly offer a treat to him through the muzzle.

These exercises/strategies will need to be repeated many times over many months to form good and positive associations with visitors. The aim is to re-train your dog to understand that visitors are a good thing. Your dog will become less anxious when guests come to the house and may even start to look forward to them. If your dog remains totally incident free for three months, the goal (if you and the visitor are brave enough to risk it) is for your dog to be un-muzzled and unsecured on the hook, unbothered by, and calm in, the presence of visitors.

# MEDICAL INTERVENTION?

I would recommend that you always speak to your veterinarian about your dog's anxiety and aggression towards strangers. To help with changing your dog's aggression towards people, your vet may consider two options:

a. Traditional medication to calm your dog. The vet may consider a prescription for selective serotonin reuptake inhibitors (SSRIs), which could be helpful – at least until the anxiety towards people reduces to a more manageable level through behavioural work and the strategies advised above. SSRIs are used for treating anxiety and fear states, obsessive-compulsive disorders, phobias and some forms of aggression. They are like the human drug Prozac. If your dog's aggression is severe and intense, medication may be helpful during desensitisation and counterconditioning strategies.

b. Complementary therapies. There is considerable anecdotal evidence to suggest that dog-appeasing pheromones (Adaptil is a well-known brand name) or Bach flower remedies could help with your dog's general anxiety of strangers. Whilst these can be purchased freely online, it's always best to let the vet know so that your dog's medical records are complete.

An alternative complementary therapy, of which many speak highly, is CBD oil, which helps reduce a dog's anxiety level. Since aggression is rooted in anxiety, CBD oils may be helpful. A veterinarian will be able to advise on quality of oils, potential side effects, specifics of dosage, lack of data and regulation.

# AGGRESSION TOWARDS OTHER DOGS

Leash reactivity in the form of a dog lunging towards and barking at other dogs is the most common form of 'aggression' complained of by owners. It is not only likely to be frightening, a cause for concern and stressful for other dogs and their owners, but also stressful for the reactive dog and their owner.

These displays of aggression towards other dogs whilst on leash, especially when it happens regardless of sex, size or breed, tend to be caused by stress – which in turn, is caused by strong emotions, high arousal levels or stimuli the dog finds unpleasant. **Fear, anxiety or anger are often the root cause** of stress and therefore on-leash aggression/reactivity.

Initially, aggressive displays are reflexive. However, dogs quickly learn that the strategy works – the aggression is rewarded by he other dog moving away and the stress of the encounter being avoided. Over repeated occasions, the aggressive response not only becomes well established but the default position of the dog, and he becomes less and less fearful and more and more assertive, sure he will succeed in forcing the other dog away.

This certainly applied in a recent case of mine. Through classical conditioning, a Leonberger had become fearful of small dogs. It all started with the fear becoming ingrained in an intense single-event learning experience of a Chihuahua latching onto her neck hair during her critical fear period between the age of 6 and 14 months. Subsequently, the experience had intensified with further exposures to the conditioned stimulus (small dogs). However, at the time I saw the client, the dog was no longer fearful after reinforcement of relief (endogenous and exogenous) through numerous successful attempts at keeping the originally feared smaller dogs away.

There are several reasons why dogs become stressed and display aggressive behaviours whilst on leash:

1. Leashes interfere with a dog's normal social interaction. This can lead to anxiety as they are unable to act naturally or exercise choice whilst on a leash. Their body language becomes stifled and stilted and because the dog can't, for example, move away should he want to do so or approach the other dog in a banana shape, he often deals with the consequent anxiety and stress by resorting to growling, lunging, snapping, etc., to force the other dog away.

2. When the situation is already tense, simple tightening of the leash can tip a dog over the edge. Sometimes, an opposition reflex (where a dog naturally pulls against the pressure from the lead holding him back) comes into play. This further increases frustration and arousal of the dog. Remember, additional arousal in aggression cases must be avoided. Furthermore, pulling against the lead also causes the dog's body posture (and therefore language) to change, making him appear aggressive and further aggravating a tense situation. In aggression cases, therefore, tension on the leash must be avoided.

3. Leash restraint frustration. This is often a result of the dog being prevented from meeting another dog and is particularly prevalent in dogs that have low impulse control or a low tolerance for frustration. The restraint can cause the dog to become highly aroused and frustrated when his desire to greet another dog is thwarted. This, in turn, can lead to anger, which leads to aggressive outlets such as barking, lunging, growling and biting.

4. The owner feels stressed. Dogs are not only familiar with the way we naturally move whilst in a relaxed state; they are sensitive to variations in the norm. When you see another dog, several things are likely to happen. Your muscles will tense slightly and your walk will change. Your breathing and heartbeat will quicken. You will release stress hormones including cortisol and adrenaline. And, guess what? Your superhuman friend is likely to notice these changes and will start to wonder if there really is a threat that is

making you uncomfortable. The dog's response is then to bark and lunge even more. It's as if a dog's lead is an umbilical cord between the owner and the dog: emotions felt by the owner travel down the lead and affect the dog.

5. Prior negative associations with events that happened on leash – e.g., prior aversive therapies, such as being shouted at when reacting or having his lead yanked. We discussed this in previous chapters. Certainly, this was the case for a client I saw recently. The owner's response to his dog's reactivity consisted of yanking her lead. This led the dog to escalate her aggression towards small dogs, to make them go away and avoid the aversive lead yanking from the owner (two-stage learning).

6. Fear and anxiety originating from a traumatic experience can lead to stress and consequent aggression when faced with a similar situation. You may not even be aware of any such trauma, but there may have been incidents so minor in your mind as to go unnoticed but by which your dog has been affected.

7. Fear and anxiety originating from the dog simply not having been adequately socialised with other dogs, particularly during puppyhood.

## WHAT'S GOING ON IN THE DOG'S MIND?

The way a dog's mind works regarding aggression towards other dogs is pretty much the same as with aggression towards people. But it's worth repeating here in case you're too lazy to flick back to the answer in the previous section!

Whilst there are several factors that can cause on-lead aggression, as discussed above, it's commonly rooted in fear that developed through a frightening and traumatic experience. The motivation behind the barking and lunging is to gain safety, the function of the behaviour is to create distance, and the reinforcement of it is the relief felt once the distance is achieved and the stress (and consequent releases of cortisol, adrenaline and other hormones) caused by the encounter abates. The distance is created either by you moving your normally angelic dog away or the owner of the targeted dog moving away. It is this relief and the consequential release of endogenous opioids that is predicted by dopamine.

# HOW TO RESOLVE AGGRESSION TOWARDS OTHER DOGS

It is worth mentioning that eliminating dog aggression can be quite difficult. This is partly because most owners find it difficult to create opportunities to practise strategies on willing dog owners. Additionally, other dogs can make the environment unstable and incendiary and ruin all the best laid plans by behaving in unpredictable ways.

To change your dog's aggressive behaviours to more acceptable behaviours, it is important to ensure that from hereon in, each new experience with other dogs that he accumulates is positive. In due course, your dog should learn to tolerate other dogs much better than he does currently, and his aggressive behaviour will be substantially reduced.

If your dog has already tasted the heat of battle and bitten, I would warn that, realistically, it may not be possible to totally remove the potential for biting and his desire to fight with another dog to resurface during a perfect storm. If your dog has bitten before, **the best way forward is often to avoid socialising your dog with dogs he is known to dislike.** Owners of such dogs will always need to be alert to such a possibility of aggression but should ensure their concern is not transmitted to their dog. In cases of dogs with a previous history of biting or a genetic makeup which often means they are more likely to perceive other dogs as threatening (for example, terriers) I would also recommend acclimatising your dog to wearing a muzzle – certainly until there has been no worrying behaviour for several months. However, bear in mind that an aggressive behaviour displayed by your dog could, in a particular situation, be totally warranted and therefore well within the range of normality.

As with changing aggression behaviours towards people, the principles of desensitisation, counterconditioning and operant conditioning are helpful when it comes to changing your dog's aggression towards other dogs when it is without provocation and is founded in fear or anxiety. Once again, we'll work outside your dog's worry zone and in his safe zone. Once again, we'll start implementation of the strategies in new places where your dog has no prior negative associations. And once again, the exposure to other dogs should use 'a hierarchy ranging from the least to the most problematical situation'.[19] You should practise bursts of brief exposure (e.g., ten seconds) at long distances for short durations (five-minute sessions advised) with breaks of around 30 seconds between each exposure. Gradually and at your dog's pace, you should build up to longer exposures (e.g., a minute), shorter distances and longer durations (e.g., 20-minute sessions) – again with 30-second breaks between exposures. Over time, your dog's worry zone should decrease and his safe zone should increase.

The first set of steps is as follows:

• To start with, select a suitably stable and confident dog to practise with in an open space without the distraction of other dogs. Enlist the owner's help by asking him to stay in one place.

• Desensitisation and counterconditioning techniques are the same when dealing with dog-on-dog aggression as when dealing with dogs displaying aggression towards members of the public. In other words, let your dog see the other dog outside his worry zone where he is calm and shows no nervous behaviour. When he looks at the other dog, mark that behaviour by telling him 'good boy' or 'yes' and give him a treat. In due course, your dog will start to look at you each time he sees a dog (because he knows other dogs mean treats). At the same time, your dog is also learning the alternative behaviour of focusing on you rather than barking at other dogs, which is a behaviour you want. Eventually, the alternative rewarded behaviour should become the default behaviour. This is known as differential reinforcement of alternative behaviours.

• Alternatively, at a distance where your dog is comfortable (in his safe zone) and whilst on lead, let him see the dog. Any behaviour other than a reactive behaviour gets a treat. This is known as differential reinforcement of other behaviours. Remember, the safe zone is your friend; the worry zone must be always avoided

• Walk across the park to the volunteer dog several times. Lessen the distance each time you walk across the park, treating your dog regularly when he sees the other dog but shows no reaction, and then walk away again. Extending distances like this means the dog is further rewarded for not showing any aggressive behaviours and remaining calm.

---

19      Burch, M. R. and Bailey, J. S. (1999) *How dogs learn*. USA: Wiley Publishing, p. 90.

- You can also try walking past the volunteer dog, ensuring you keep the volunteer dog in your dog's safe zone for a few minutes. If your dog looks at you or shows no overreaction to the dog or remains calm and relaxed, he should be rewarded.

- Over a period of weeks, when sufficiently comfortable with walking by in this way with different confident and well-socialised dogs, both dogs can walk across the park at decreasing distances from each other – but always outside your dog's worry zone. This outcome should be rewarded.

- Try walking behind the other dog whilst treating your dog so that he builds positive associations towards the smell of the other dog.

- Mix walking with sitting on a bench with both dogs on leads, keeping the other dog in your dog's safe zone. Progress to reducing the distance, depending on how your dog and the other dog are faring.

- Repeat the above steps regularly on as many days and in different parks and places as possible with different stable subject dogs.

- How quickly you move on to the second set of steps set out below, will depend on how quickly progress is made towards both dogs being totally calm around each other. Please note the type of body language that conveys a dog being comfortable as set out in Chapter 8.

- Until your dog's on-leash aggression has improved and his worry zone has reduced to a radius of around two or three metres, you should avoid dogs whose temperaments are unknown and the types of dogs your dog just doesn't get on with.

- During these steps, you must be careful not to get to a distance that will provoke a response from your dog or the other dog. If there is any response from either dog, calmly extend the distance and/or redirect your dog to focus on you ('watch me'). As soon as your dog is calm, he should be treated and the exercise ended.

- You should always be matter-of-fact about extending the distance. There should be no shouting, or snap-checking the lead, or any other action that could be construed by your dog as anything other than complete calmness and confidence on your part.

- My preference is that you avoid on-leash introductions totally. If you can't adhere to this advice, at the very least ensure that you never exert any leash tension whilst there is an on-leash introduction. This, however, is almost certainly impossible for most people.

- When the other dog is not present, treats should stop.

The aim of this first set of steps is to help your dog understand that whenever he sees and calmly walks near or is near another dog, he gets treats and that generally, the experience is a good one. When, and only when, your dog becomes more relaxed by this realisation and his worry zone has been reduced to two to three metres, you can progress to the next part of the programme.

The second set of steps is as follows:

• Whilst still on leash, initially begin parallel walking with sufficient distance between the dogs that no uncomfortable response is provoked from either dog, and then parallel walk closer. This step must only be taken if there was calmness and the absence of any aggressive signals on the part of your dog and the stooge dog during the first steps above. Please refer to Chapter 8 on what calmness might look like.

• Keep the dogs on leads for a couple of hundred yards, and if both dogs remain totally calm, then progress to walking off leash. There should be no trouble at this stage. If there is any hint of either dog tensing, call your dog, treat him, and end the session.

• Keep the play session short. Give it a few minutes, then treat and repeat another time.

Other helpful steps are as follows:

• If you can't find a volunteer owner and dog, you could sit alone with your dog on lead in a public area watching other dogs go by in his safe zone, rewarding your dog when there is no reaction from him.

• Should your dog be on leash and an unplanned off-leash dog comes toward you, you should walk the other way, throwing a handful of food treats towards the other dog. Whilst the other dog is enjoying your top-quality treats, it should allow you to escape. Alternatively, to avoid escalation of aggression with a persistent off-lead dog, if you have an umbrella with you, open that as a barrier between the other dog and your dog. That may help the unleashed dog return to his owner or go elsewhere.

• Should your dog be off leash, and an unplanned on-leash dog comes toward you, you should ask your dog to 'stay' or call him back and then put him on a lead. If you do not have this level of control over your dog, you are not ready to have your dog off leash in an environment where you and your dog might come a cropper.

• If your dog does react, or has encountered stressful situations prior to implementing the behaviour modification strategies, try the training another day. This is because of what is sometimes referred to as trigger stacking. This is all about your dog releasing cortisol (a stress hormone) each time he has a stressful encounter. Because it takes many hours for cortisol levels to reduce to normal after encountering a stressor, cortisol released from new stressful encounters combines with the levels from previous encounters. Your dog's fuse gets shorter and shorter and a new minor encounter (that in the absence of previous stressful encounters might not have caused your dog to react aggressively) can easily push him over the edge of his threshold. For this reason, end the exercise, don't begin the exercise, or at the very least, be aware that a previous worry zone of 40 feet might now actually be 80 feet. Remember, once a dog tips over his threshold, he can't think logically and you won't be able to reason with him. In short, the modification programme above requires the implementation of two sets of steps. The first involves rewarding your dog at distances that do not evoke an aggressive response from him. The second builds up to letting your dog off the lead once he has become desensitised and counterconditioned to other dogs and is comfortable with the subject dog at close distances.

**Of paramount importance is this: all and any non-aggressive behaviour MUST be regularly rewarded by you.** Positive reinforcement will soon impact on your dog's behaviour as he comes to realise that other dogs are not to be feared and indeed being around them is a rewarding and pleasant experience. This is counterconditioning. Operant conditioning is also involved, as we reinforce the dog whenever he looks at the dog and offers an alternative behaviour, such as looking at you or doing anything other than being aggressive.

**At no stage should your dog be reprimanded for aggressive behaviour. This will not help in the long term and certainly does not teach him the required behaviour.**

In addition, if your dog's aggression is intense and his worry zone is much bigger than 100 feet, you should consider asking for veterinarian involvement in either prescribing medication or at least advising on the use of complementary therapies to help in your dog's aggression behaviour modification, as previously discussed.

# RESOURCE GUARDING

This is all about dogs not wanting to give up something that they value when a person approaches or attempts to take that thing away. What follows are aggressive behaviours that might include growling, lunging and even biting.

What the resource actually is can vary. It might be a food bowl, a chew, a toy, a place or even a person. In certain circumstances, for example, a dog might not let you come near your partner while sitting on the sofa. Your dog might only guard your partner on a particular sofa. The possibilities are endless.

When dogs exhibit aggressive behaviours around things, it's often referred to as **resource guarding** or **possessive aggression**. If the aggressive behaviours arise around edible things only, it's sometimes referred to as **food-related aggression**. However, dogs can display threatening behaviours even if they are not in possession of the resource. In 'dog law', it's not just what's in their mouth/in their possession that is theirs; it can be a resource they value that is in their vicinity. In this book, I'll use the above terms interchangeably.

Resource guarding discussed in this chapter is distinct from dogs displaying agonistic behaviours for other reasons. Here are two examples:

- Aggression that arises as a result of being protective of an owner can look like a dog resource guarding a person, but the difference is that the aggressive behaviour by the dog appears to be activated when the dog perceives his owner to be under threat. The behaviour displayed is generally a movement towards the threat and the dog positioning himself between the owner and the approaching person. With resource guarding, however, the dog generally, though not always, stays in place, protecting his resource, or moves away with the resource. Specific breeds, such as Dobermans and German shepherds may display protective behaviours more than other breeds. However, protective behaviour is by no means restricted to a specific breed.

- Aggression caused by physical contact between the owner and another person, e.g., hugging or kissing, involves the dog attempting to separate the parties by getting in between them, barking and or jumping up at them.

There are several reasons why dogs become possessive about resources and resource guarding behaviours occur.

First, **the behaviour can be learned during puppyhood** by breeders not managing the dog's learning as well as they might. Puppies learn resource guarding from their mother or littermates. Even at a few weeks of age, breeders have noted puppies growling during food time – a very natural behaviour.

Secondly, **we are often a major cause of reinforcing aggressive behaviours** when a dog is guarding resources. In the dog's mind, the thought process is the same for both aggression over food and possessive aggression over other items, whether they're toys or other household items. The scenario goes like this:

- The dog has possession of a valued resource.
- The resource is regularly taken from him by the owner (often through intimidation tactics) with no benefit to the dog in return.
- Whilst the dog is a puppy, he may be cowed and relinquish the resource.
- As the dog grows older and develops confidence, he signals to the owner that he is not comfortable with the situation.
- If the owner persists in taking things away, the dog escalates his displeasure signal by snarling or snapping. This behaviour normally causes most owners to back off.
- Each battle won by the dog reinforces the dog's behaviour; the behaviour has worked and there is no reason for him to change it.

Of course, it isn't sensible to meet the dog's aggression with aggression of our own. That only serves to escalate the concern and aggression on the dog's part.

Thirdly, the practice advocated by some trainers of **removing a dog's food bowl while he is eating or forcefully taking a resource through intimidating tactics**, can cause anxiety leading to displays of aggression and guarding.

It is difficult for some owners to see the benefit of positive reinforcement in teaching their dog to voluntarily give up resources. Instead, such owners can resort to taking things from the dog through intimidation. Whilst your dog may cower and give up a resource during his puppy phase in response to intimidation tactics, he is certainly likely to begin to put up a fight and start resource guarding once he begins to mature. In 1998, the Canadian Hospitals Injury

Reporting and Prevention Program published the results of dog bite reports in Canada in 1996. The data identified that dog bites are often associated with playing with, feeding or hurting (or 'disciplining') the dog and due to misinterpreting or misunderstanding warning signals exhibited by the dog.

Finally, **arrival of a new dog into the house** can be the match that ignites the resource guarding nature of some dogs. This can cause arguments between the dogs over resources, including people. If the resource guarding is not nipped in the bud using positive reinforcement and environmental management, the resource guarding behaviour becomes learnt and ingrained.

## WHAT'S GOING ON IN THE DOG'S MIND?

Dogs follow dog law: that which is in their possession is theirs. The dog's motivation is to maintain possession – signalled by stillness, a direct stare at the owner, and various other signals discussed in Chapter 8. These signals come well before the growling, lunging and biting. The function of these signals is to create distance, and the behaviour is reinforced by the relief that comes when the owner moves away. The motivation for the behaviour largely comes from the dog wanting to retain the comfort value of the item.

When you ignore your dog's very clear signals, your dog feels anxious and frustrated, potentially activating (if you subscribe to the classical view of emotions – see Chapter 3) the rage system and causing him to growl. Whilst essentially a negative effect, following successes in keeping the owner away, rage can have a positive effect for the dog and so aggression becomes learned – and becomes a behaviour the dog is likely to repeat.

Of course, if you subscribe to the constructed view of emotions, the dog will view you and your approach as thoroughly unpleasant and will become highly aroused as you continue with your approach. Then, based on past experiences as a guide, he is likely to be aggressive.

Either way, the dog's motivation is to maintain possession. The function of the aggressive behaviour, though chiefly to create distance, could also involve an element of making contact, with additional reinforcement coming from the release of frustration in making contact.

Whether your dog views you as something unpleasant or whether the rage system is activated, there will be releases of certain chemicals. These include testosterone, substance P, norepinephrine, glutamate and other chemicals. The ultimate reinforcement is the deactivation of the negative and unpleasant affective rage circuitry (classical view) or reduction of arousal levels and the unpleasantness of your approach (constructed view) and reversion to a calm state. That calm state leads to the release of endogenous opioids, which makes your dog feel good.

In addition, where owners have used force (rather than positive reinforcement) to take items from their dog, it is likely that the dog considers the owner as an aversive and fears that he may be punished for taking possession of an item when they approach him. As such, fuelled by endogenous catecholamines, CRF, cortisol, other neuropeptides and glutamate, the fear system may become activated. This, in turn, is likely to lead to aggression motivated by the desire to avoid the negative effect of FEAR and the need to feel safe. Dopamine release will predict reinforcement and the owner moving away. In these circumstances, the function of the aggression is to maintain a distance the dog considers safe and the reinforcement for the behaviour comes when the distance is achieved, with the consequent release of endogenous opioids and dopamine.

This scenario was mirrored by a client of mine recently. He used to forcefully take things from his dog, including through reprimands. The dog came to regard the client as a punisher and had learned and feared that the client's approach meant further aversive actions and that, frustratingly, items would be taken from her. The dog's growling, having succeeded in keeping the client away, had resulted in the dog continuing with and escalating her strategy. The client had felt that the dog's growling was a display of dominance. In this regard, the client was labouring under a misapprehension. He was simply misinterpreting the dog's fear signals, e.g., whale eyes, anxiety signals of lip licking, paw lifts, etc., and warning signals, including a lowered head, tight closed mouth, nose pointing to the resource and eyes at the owner, as dominance aggression. During confrontational approaches, the dog in fact became more stressed, causing a release of chemicals including cortisol. This in turn lowered the dog's threshold for responding reactively and aggressively which in turn inhibited her rational capacity.

*Frank – resource guarding.*

In conclusion, resource guarding is often a result of a history of resources having been taken away from the dog. Negative associations have developed in the dog's mind, and often, the dog will fear a person approaching him whilst he has a resource.

Resource guarding can have an impact on the whole family. Owners can become afraid of their dog. In addition, there can be an emotional impact when one partner is unable to sit next to the other.

Any behaviour change strategy should involve rebuilding relationships between the dog and the owners. This can be done through play with the dog, training, and other fun activities in environments that do not involve any resource guarding.

## HOW TO RESOLVE RESOURCE GUARDING – CHEWS, FOOD, TOYS, STOLEN HOUSEHOLD ITEMS

The strategies I have used with clients and Frank with great success involve teaching your dog to trust you around his food bowl, chews or household possessions and convincing the dog that giving up the item or you being near the item means something good will happen and certainly nothing bad, and that you are not a threat or competition. A good book to read is *How Dogs Learn* by Mary R. Burch and Jon S. Bailey. In addition, there is a useful article by S. Gibeault, 'How to Teach Your Dog to Drop It'.[20]

20      Gibeault, S. (2020) 'How to Teach Your Dog to Drop It.' *American Kennel Club*. Available from https://www.akc.org/expert-advice/training/teaching-your-dog-to-drop-it/

The aim of the two-stage action plan below is to countercondition your dog's current thinking that you appearing near his food bowl predicts that something bad will happen – namely his existing fear and anxiety in the face of you approaching whilst he is in possession of an item. A process of slow desensitisation is also used to gradually accustom your dog to you approaching him and to extinguish his fear response.

Before discussing the action plan, remember:

- Do not try to take the food, chew or item from your dog.
- Do not threaten or shout at your dog to make him release the resource.
- Do not intimidate or dominate your dog in any way, e.g., by towering over him.
- Do not get so close to your dog that it makes him tense up or growl. Stay at a distance that provokes no reaction from your dog. In other words, outside his worry zone and in his safe zone.

### *Stage 1*

1. Set up a situation in which your dog would resource guard. You should leave the room and re-enter with a handful of your dog's favourite treats, stopping well before your dog's worry zone (let's say it's five feet) to toss a treat to him. Once your dog has eaten the tasty treat, the exercise should be repeated a few times before you leave the room. Feeding treats in this way is counterconditioning at work. The dog starts to predict that whenever you go near him, good things will come.

2. All sessions should be kept short, i.e., a minute or so, to avoid your dog becoming stressed, but should be repeated several times. If your dog leaves the guarded resource and follows you, throw a treat away from the resource, calmly pick up the resource and give it back to your dog. We want the dog to understand that him taking the treat does not equal you taking the resource away.

3. After a few sessions of this over a couple of days, you should try walking only one step closer than your dog's original threshold distance. Then toss the food treat and withdraw one step and then leave the room. If your dog gives any warning signs (e.g., stiffening body), you should start further back or only approach in half steps.

4. Gradually, over time, once your dog is content to have you close to him, you could sit next to him and place/toss treats in front

of him, but at the same time touch the treats with a finger. This habituates your dog to having your hand near the resource.

## *Stage 2*

The second stage is to use operant conditioning to teach your dog to 'drop' once Stage 1 has been successful and your dog is happy for you to sit next to him. Initially, you should use a resource of low value for this training to ensure lower arousal levels rather than one that evokes any resource guarding.

1. Teaching 'drop' involves a swap with something your dog finds highly reinforcing.

2. After a few seconds of play with an item of low value, you should hold the treat in front of his nose or drop it in front of his nose. Once your dog drops the item to take the treat, you must praise and then give the (or if dropped on the floor, another) treat. You should then cue your dog to take the item again. This way, your dog is rewarded again and you've helped him understand that even if he drops the resource, you have no intention of taking it.

3. Repeat the process regularly and often, and when your dog is totally comfortable with your hand being near the resource, you can slowly (watching out for the dog being concerned about this) and calmly pick up the resource and give it back to your dog as soon as he has finished the treat.

4. Once your dog reliably drops the item as soon as you show the treat, a verbal cue of 'drop' can be added.

5. I agree with Gibeault's suggestion that after several repetitions, the lure should be faded out and the cue given without showing the treats. If your dog doesn't drop the item without seeing the treats, you should wait one second between the cue and showing the treat. You should slowly increase that time across repetitions until your dog understands to drop the item before the treats come out

6. In due course, you should practise with more and more valuable resources. It is important to repeat that you should take your time in increasing the value of the resource when practising the above actions. At the time I started writing this book, Frank found it impossible to relinquish a raw chicken wing, and it seemed he might never get there. However, I'm pleased to report that after months of consistent practice, Frank will now (with a little reluctance) drop

even chicken wings when asked. What a good boy he is. So, it is crucial that we first practice with low value resources and help the dog understand that our approach does not mean we will take it away.

I should mention that sometimes, the resource guarding behaviour becomes so ingrained in a dog's mind it becomes difficult to change. Sometimes, it is difficult for owners to find the time to consistently practise the strategies outlined here because it can take months to change a dog's mindset. It took Frank eight months for him to comfortably relinquish, for example, a sock that he might have picked up. For dogs in this situation, it is often best to manage the environment and prevent access to items they are apt to guard, such as toys. Alternatively, it might be easier to prevent access to the dog whilst he is, for example, eating.

## HOW TO RESOLVE RESOURCE GUARDING – PEOPLE

When a dog is resource guarding a person, he'll display threatening behaviour, often through growling, when approached whilst sitting near the person he's guarding.

The strategies and steps involved are the same as those discussed above for when a dog is resource guarding a chew or toy, and involve counterconditioning and reinforcing non-aggressive behaviours

## ACTION PLAN

1. Let the dog sit next to the owner he is apt to guard (Owner A).

2. The other owner/person (Owner B) should walk past the dog at a comfortable distance and gently toss him a treat.

3. Repeat step 2 many times, over many sessions, over many days, and perhaps weeks.

4. Look for body language that tells you the dog is more comfortable with Owner B's approach and passing by. You're after more relaxed ears, mouth and body as opposed to a closed tight mouth, a fixed stare and tense body. Please see Chapter 8 for more on this.

5. Owner B should approach and drop the treat for the dog from different angles, in different rooms and at different times of the day.

6. Owner A, sitting next to the dog, may also feed treats whilst Owner B is approaching and passing by.

7. To ensure the safety of all, it may be appropriate to muzzle the dog, have him on a lead or even behind a gate/pen. This depends entirely on the precise circumstances of your case.

8. When the dog is comfortable being approached from different angles and at different speeds, the distances can be reduced and Owner B may be able to walk by at very close distances or even stand still near the dog whilst administering treats before walking off again.

9. In due course, the dog will learn that the approach of owner B predicts good things happening rather than bad things happening such as the dog losing his place or losing Owner A. Once the dog shows totally comfortable body language in close proximity to Owner B, Owner B may be able to sit next to the dog and Owner A. Before doing this, it may be appropriate for Owner A to move further away from the dog or to totally leave the sofa and re-join the dog and Owner B a few seconds later.

10. Interspersed with the above action plan, recalls can also be practised by Owner B whilst the dog is sitting next to Owner A. It is important to allow the dog back onto the sofa after he has gone to Owner B for a treat. This will help him understand that leaving the guarded Owner A after being recalled by Owner B does not mean that his place on the sofa is lost. If the dog is called and a treat is thrown on the floor away from the sofa, Owner B may sit on the sofa, then allow the dog back onto the sofa whilst Owner B leaves again.

11. Generally, teach the dog to relax at a distance away from the person he is apt to guard.

# AGGRESSION BETWEEN FAMILY DOGS

Infighting between two family dogs is hugely stressful for both the dogs and the family. It's distressing for the dogs because they are confined together by brick walls and tight spaces and constantly encounter stressful situations they can't escape to do what they do best – lead a dog's life without any worries or strife. It's distressing for owners because, often, the two dogs will have historically got on wonderfully and without any squabbles. Then, within weeks or even days of the initial growl or posturing, the dogs are literally at each other's throats. Not only is it distressing, but it's also dangerous for those owners who try to break up a fight.

Does the above sound familiar? It was certainly spot on for one of my clients. She had a boxer (let's call him C), aged three. Friendly, but boisterous. No recall, pulled on the lead like a train, and generally, the client had little control over him. She then decided that it would be a lovely idea to get a boxer puppy. They are cute, after all – who could resist? The puppy (let's call him W), was of a nervous disposition and had a low threshold to all sorts of stimuli. C had already been castrated, so the client decided to have W castrated as well, before his first birthday. Taking away W's prize jewels probably did little for his nervousness and general anxiety for the reasons discussed in Chapter 9.

Well, C and W got on brilliantly until W hit around 14 months. From then on, much blood ensued during numerous fights. The blood was not just from the dogs. The client tried several times to break up fights, and one or the other dog would redirect his aggression to her. So, she had some scars to show the children. But it was no good crying over spilled blood. It was time to act.

## WHAT'S GOING ON IN THE DOG'S MIND?

The main reason two household dogs start to fight is due to the younger dog beginning to reach social maturity. As he does so, it's common for him to start pushing boundaries so far as the older dog is concerned. The younger dog may push in to be petted first. He may try and sit closer to you or go through a doorway before the other dog. He might try to lie on the older dog's bed or stand in front of the older dog to control his movements. Some of these challenging behaviours may be overlooked by owners, but they're certainly not overlooked by the other dog. Whilst the older dog may allow a young pup to get away with some of these rude behaviours, he is unlikely to take kindly to the behaviours from a maturing dog.

Sometimes, the younger dog needs to do nothing at all. The simple fact of him beginning to reach maturity is enough for the older dog to start asserting HIS position; pre-emptive action, so to speak.

However, the root cause could be something else. That something else could be one of the causes of aggression in dogs that we covered in Chapter 4. For example, it may be some medical condition that has taken hold recently and is causing the dog to become stressed, over-reactive and aggressive. It could be an upheaval in the dogs' environment or routines that causes them a huge amount of stress. A new house move, another family dog passing away, arguments amongst the owners, a bereavement, anxiety from a family member, a new child and so on all cause a dog stress.

And what about air travel and its effects on behaviour? I am regularly instructed by clients that are constantly jetting around the globe for business and pleasure. Of course, the dogs go with them, and it has a physiological effect on them and is a hugely stressful experience, even with the use of medication to calm them.[21] [22] The

21    Bergeron, R., Scott, S. L., Emond, J.-P., Mercier, F., Cook, N. J. and Schaefer, A. L. (2002) 'Physiology and behavior of dogs during air transport.' *Canadian Journal of Veterinary Research*, vol. 66(3): 211–216.

22    Venable, E. B., Clark, S., Holscher, H. D. and Swanson, K. S. (2016) 'Effects of Air Travel on the Canine Microbiome: A Pilot Study.' *International Journal of Veterinary Health Science & Research*. doi:10.19070/2332-2748-1600028

dogs get very grotty with each other, and I can't help but notice and wonder about a link between the flight and the bouts of infighting.

Now, this squabbling between dogs is fine if the younger dog submits or the older dog accepts a change of guard. The problem arises when neither wants to give in.

## RESOLVING AGGRESSION BETWEEN FAMILY DOGS

Before we talk about what you need to do in case you find yourself in my client's shoes, let's discuss things to avoid.

## WHAT NOT TO DO

- Don't start reinforcing the most dominant dog. There are several reasons for this. First, it presupposes that that there is one dog that is always dominant. Unfortunately, that's often not true. Sometimes a dog is more dominant in one set of circumstances and the other dog in another set of circumstances.

Frank, for example, is more dominant vis-a-vis Ragnar when my daughter and her husband are around, and much more submissive when no one is around. Of course, there may be an element of resource guarding people here. There is even a difference in his behaviour based on which person is around. Frank is more assertive towards Ragnar when my wife is around, but less so when I'm around. Maybe I see the signs of Frank's dominance earlier than my wife and manage the situation better. Frank is also much more dominant around food, but Ragnar is much more assertive when it comes to toys.

Secondly, not only can specific situations determine dominance, but a dog can simply feel more assertive one day and not the next. Additionally, the whole relationship might change over the course of a few months. The dogs may have agreed this between themselves. You getting involved by trying to reinforce one dog based on your understanding of who is dominant might cause more issues by reintroducing arguments that had already been resolved between the dogs.

Finally, it is extremely difficult for most dog owners (and the average dog trainer) to correctly assess whether the dog is being dominant because he is a dominant dog or whether he's acting dominant but underneath the bravado, he is the anxious, nervous and insecure one.

• Don't punish either one of the dogs or rant, rave, and shout at them during a squabble. Remember, this sort of action by you is likely only to exacerbate an already tense situation by increasing the dogs' levels of arousal and stress. It is also crucial that you use your best endeavours not overreact to situations. Your stress and tension can be misinterpreted by one or both dogs.

• Don't attempt to break up a fight by getting in between the dogs to force them apart. We've discussed in previous chapters that when a dog's limbic system is active or when he is highly aroused, he can't really think logically. We also discussed how tightening a lead can push the dog over the edge when he is 'in conversation' with another dog. You reaching down to restrain a dog has the same effect and causes him to become even more frustrated through being prevented from continuing the heated discussion or getting to his target. He is then likely to turn round in a blind rage and literally bite the hand that feeds him. We often see this when two dogs become over-aroused and stressed by a gate preventing them from getting at a passing dog beyond the gate. What do they do? Turn on each other.

When you have dogs that have squabbled in the past, it is a good idea to be prepared if you haven't managed the environment and a fight does break out. Better options than physically breaking up the fight yourself include a bucket of water thrown over the pair, a tennis racket or broom to separate them, a heavy duvet over the pair, or an air canister or fire extinguisher. If there are two adults at home, each person holding and slightly raising the hind legs of one of the fighting dogs and then moving in clockwise fashion can also work. Whatever you do, don't use your hands to try and pry them apart when they're already fighting or whilst they're having a tense 'discussion'.

## WHAT TO DO

• Whilst infighting can be reduced through various protocols and environmental management, the truth is that sometimes it can't, and the dogs simply will not get on. It's a relationship issue. Sometimes the effort needed to manage the situation may be too herculean for your specific circumstances. These specific circumstances might include young, boisterous children in the home, your workload preventing you from being able to supervise the dogs, or the layout of your house preventing you from creating safe separate spaces for the dogs. Whatever the case, you need to think with your head and not with your heart. The risks are great, particularly with young children about who might get caught up in the middle of a fight. So, first consider whether it might be best for all concerned for one of the dogs to be rehomed, perhaps by a relative.

• The next thing on your checklist in the event of sudden aggression should be a visit to your veterinarian. One of the dogs may have arthritis and might be constantly bothered by any contact with the other dog. Even if the dogs are medically fine, medication or a natural remedy may be appropriate to help calm them. Oh yeah, did I mention dog-appeasing pheromones might be a great idea in these circumstances? Try it. It can't do any harm.

• Note the triggers that cause the posturing and fighting. Is it caused by tension over resources? This could be a chew, a toy, a place or even you! And if you are the cause of the infighting, is it because the dogs are seeing you as a resource or because you're stressed and they're picking up on that? If the triggers revolve around resources, these resources must be removed or we need to apply basic training and cue one dog go to his bed whilst the other has the resource or is given affection. They need to learn to take turns.

Sometimes, jostling through tight spaces, especially if they're both aroused due to, for example, the arrival of a guest, can cause the arousal to go through the roof and lead to a fight. Where the arrival of the postman, the Deliveroo guy dropping off your curry, or people and other dogs going by the window produces a negative conditioned emotional response, it is the adrenaline released that can push dogs over the edge and result in them turning on each other.

• You've assessed the triggers, now it's time to assess and reduce anything else in the dogs' lives that might be causing them stress and consequently lowering their threshold in regard to each other. So, longer periods of separation and short periods of union without triggers is in order. Make sure they each have their own place to sleep and rest.

If you live in a small two-up, two-down terraced house and have four children, perhaps the house is just too small and crowded for two dogs and six people! Constantly bumping into each other and not being able to get away would certainly stress out many dogs that need their own space. This was the case for my client's dogs. W suffered from high anxiety and was constantly overreacting to the slightest noise and movement. This caused stress for both the dogs, which were always close by.

In conjunction with reducing stress, put your dogs in a better mood by ensuring you are meeting their three essential needs: physical, emotional, and mental and environmental stimulation (see Chapter 5).

• Supervise the dogs with your body and mind. Don't try to multitask by working or looking after the children at the same time as trying to supervise the dogs. If you can't do this, manage the environment to keep them apart, especially where stressors/triggers are present. To prevent the dogs arguing over resources, let them take turns being with you or near a resource. This may mean using physical barriers. Baby gates are ideal as they allow the dogs to see each other, and for us to see signs of relaxation; at which stage we can reward those relaxed behaviours to help the dogs understand the behaviours we like and want.

Managing the environment may also mean that until and unless we have achieved our aim of both dogs being able to coexist in the same room without squabbling, you should acclimatise both to wearing muzzles.

• Train your dogs to listen to you. If they don't listen to you, ask yourself why. One of the reasons dogs don't listen to us, as mentioned in Chapter 2, is likely to apply and must be addressed.

There are several useful cues you should teach them, especially if you are the trigger for their squabbling. Teaching them to sit or lie on their beds is crucial for when both dogs are in the room and you want them to calmly take turns in, for example, taking a treat from you or being petted by you. Crucially, this also helps keep their arousal levels in check.

This training will help the dogs to live in harmony in your house. The training will also bring calmness by taking the stress out of having to work out what they can and can't get away with. So, it is important to practice stroking one dog whilst the other is lying calmly on his bed or sitting at a distance that is not going to over arouse him, rather than at such a short distance apart where he finds it impossible to keep his bottom on the floor. Then rotate. Ask both to sit a distance apart from each other and treat each one in turn. Over time, distances can be decreased as you take it in turn to treat them. If there are any signs of over arousal, the distances need to be increased again – you are likely moving too fast for the dogs.

• Keep their arousal levels in check by training them to greet you politely and put an end to boisterous behaviour. This is easy. Dogs are only boisterous when they are rewarded whilst in a boisterous state. Ignore them and calmly pet them when they are calm. Also, keep their arousal levels in check by providing them with a set of rules, regulations and boundaries. The home is no place for tear-arsing around and using the furniture as a high-energy playground.

• Help your dogs to keep stress at bay by regularly giving them their own space and only putting them with each other for very brief periods, and only then whilst under your supervision. Separating them for lengthy periods is particularly important after they have squabbled. Remember cortisol and adrenaline can stay in your dog's system for hours or days. A reintroduction whilst still fuelled by cortisol and adrenaline will mean that they will react to each other for even a minor misdemeanour.

• Desensitise and counter-condition the dogs so they are calm and comfortable in each other's presence in the face of potential triggers, rather than reacting aggressively. Counterconditioning will also help the dogs to view each other's presence as predicting something pleasant.

We've discussed these principles before. If the dogs are becoming aggressive during possession of a toy or food when the other dog is around, this could be dealt with in the following way:

1. Secure one of the dogs (A) on a lead in one part of the room with a toy, or food in a Kong.

2. Walk by with the other dog (B), also on leash.

3. Each time you walk by with B, throw a treat to A. This treat needs to be of higher value than the toy or food in the Kong. Whilst you're at it, treat B as well for not reacting, or to keep his attention on you rather than A.

4. Repeat this for a couple of minutes.

5. Over several sessions, the aim is to reduce the distance between the dogs as you walk by, but to always remain in A's safe zone (outside his worry zone). If the worry zone is bigger than the room, then

put the dogs in separate rooms divided by a baby gate. Reward the dogs whenever they're in a relaxed state.

6. Over time, you can stand around with B whilst you treat both dogs.

The idea is to get the dogs comfortable around each other and in the presence of some minor triggers. Ultimately, you may be able to reach the point where both dogs can have their own chews whilst in their respective safe zones. But this would certainly be an exercise that needs to be supervised. It is not advised that you leave the dogs with chews whilst you go AWOL.

With lots of micro-management of spaces and places, training, ensuring stressors that trigger the aggression are reduced to a minimum, desensitising and counterconditioning the dogs' behaviour in relation to any stressors that can't be removed, the aggression should lessen to manageable levels. If the aggression remains and your dogs just can't abide each other, you may only have three options available to you – none of which are easy to take. Either the dogs should never see each other and are managed in such a way that they live in different parts of the home, or are constantly muzzled, or one or the other is rehomed. On the odd occasion, however, euthanisation of one dog, as a last resort, has finally provided peace for all concerned.

# PULLING ON THE LEAD

Most dogs pull on the lead because they've never actually been taught not to. It is prevalent when a dog is excited – for example, on the way to the park and not on the way back home. This makes the dog walking experience unpleasant for both dog and owner.

In conjunction with pulling, most clients report that their dog insists on continuously meandering on walks, taking every opportunity to stop and sniff his surroundings whenever he chooses. It is normal and healthy for dogs to sniff the environment because it passes a whole host of information to the dog. However, excessive sniffing at the dog's behest can be tiresome for the owner. Whilst we do not want to stop dogs exploring the environment, it is quite appropriate to help them understand that when the lead is attached, they must not pull this way and that to sniff this and that.

Why do they pull to start with? Well, partly because dogs naturally walk and go round exploring the world much faster than us. In addition to that, the environment is constantly beckoning the dog to explore it and read all the pee-mails left by other dogs. Finally, each time the dog gets to explore the environment through pulling, the behaviour is reinforced and so it continues. Remember, even if you manage to walk your dog on a loose leash 90% of the time, when he manages to succeed in moving forward even 10% of the time, that pulling is likely to be reinforced on a variable ratio schedule of reinforcement.

*Ragnar showing Frank how to walk on a loose leash.*

So, if you're teaching a dog to walk on a loose leash, you now know never to walk even one step whilst there is tension in the lead. Luckily, there are lots of things you can do if there's tension in the lead as you start to walk.

# HOW TO STOP YOUR DOG PULLING ON THE LEASH

## GENERAL ADVICE

- Start off in the home and then the garden, where there are few or no distractions. Remember the three Ds (distraction, distance and duration) and the other training tips discussed in Chapter 6.
- Once heel/loose leash walking has been mastered at home and in the garden, then practise and master it in quiet areas, unknown to the dog, with no distractions.
- Once loose lead walking has been mastered in unknown and quiet areas, practise in areas with increasing distractions.
- Don't leave the house until your dog is sitting or standing calmly. If he's super aroused before you even step out of the house, the arousal levels are only going north once you're outside.
- Praise should be given in a soft, gentle voice.
- Practising in unknown areas may help to keep your dog's focus on you more than it might in an area where he's used to meeting his mates and running to them, or there are various other distractions he's become accustomed to running towards.
- The lead should be no longer than a standard six-foot lead.

## SPECIFIC ACTIONS

- As soon as the dog is more than two feet or so ahead of you and there's tension in the leash, walk in the opposite direction. Tell him 'good boy' as he follows and then passes you to create tension in the leash again. Walk in the opposite direction as soon as there is tension in the leash again, and keep repeating.
- The pulling should become less intense as your dog gets to the end of the leash, knowing you'll be going in the opposite direction

- Alternatively, when your dog pulls, stop (you should call him to you if he doesn't turn round of his own accord to wonder why you've applied the brakes). Move forwards only when the leash is loose.

- You should also stop and start regularly whether he's pulling on the lead or not. He should soon begin to wonder what the idiot at the end of the lead (you) is doing and start focusing on staying with you on a loose leash.

- Reward your dog on a regular basis when he is walking on a loose leash.

- To complement the stopping and starting strategy, throw in going in the opposite direction and walking in a haphazard manner, rather than in a straight line: left, right, back, forward, anticlockwise and clockwise and so on.

- Whilst you're at it, also try walking at different speeds rather than always at the same speed. Your dog needs to learn to walk at your pace, not his

- Do not stop walking at the behest of your dog – for example, when he wants to stop to sniff. A gentle 'let's go' and keep walking and treat. But do go back to the spot he wanted to sniff and, at your instigation, stop regularly to let him sniff.

- When walking down a narrow alley or a walled/hedged pathway, you should ensure your dog is slightly behind you. Use your leg/body to prompt him not to rush forwards. This will help him walk behind you and help him understand loose leash walking.

- If you happen upon some bollards, use the opportunity to weave in and out – make it fun. Your dog will start to focus on you.

- Incorporate a play period at the end of each training session.

- Remember to praise your dog on a regular basis.

- Another game you can play to help him walk on a loose leash is to place a couple of treats at your feet and as your dog hoovers them up, walk forward two steps and place a couple more at your feet for him. Continue to repeat for 100 yards, altering the timing of placing the treats at your feet. Your dog shouldn't have pulled, and he'll start to get the hang of not pulling.

- Alternatively, offer him a treat after one step, then after two steps, then after three steps and so on. Your dog should start focusing on you as he waits for his treat. See how many steps you can walk whilst he's focused on you before he starts to think about pulling. It's a start to teaching him to focus on and stay with you rather than surging forward. Whilst he's focusing on you, throw in the stopping and starting, walking in a haphazard manner and walking at different speeds.

• Another way of helping a dog learn how to walk on a loose leash, is to walk him with a dog that is already adept at this. This strategy certainly helped Frank. Dogs are good at learning by copying their peers.

These practice sessions need to be repeated regularly and often, in different locations and situations so that the dog understands that whenever the lead is attached, moving forwards only occurs when the lead is loose.

In due course, the aim is for your dog to walk next to you even when he is not leashed. When practising this, start with the lead still attached, but draped over his back so he knows the lead is still on. Over time, the lead can be removed and your dog should, with a bit of prompting if needed, stay close to you and assume a loose leash walking position.

# JUMPING UP

Licking is a normal behaviour between dogs. It's a sign of deference. Mouths are a funfair of interesting smells, tastes and information for them. When translated to human interaction, the height difference between humans and dogs leads to the associated practice of jumping up. If you moved around your house on all fours, your dog probably would never need to jump up to reach your mouth.

Whilst jumping up is cute during puppyhood, it's not so cute when the dog is older, dirty or jumping up at someone who doesn't appreciate it. Perhaps that someone, dare I say it, doesn't like dogs or is frightened of them.

We reinforce the behaviour when the dog's a puppy, and then we complain about it. How frustrating and confusing for dogs.

How did we reinforce the behaviour in the first place? Well, what's the first thing you did when your puppy came home and you quite rightly, sat on the floor to pet him? He probably put his front paws on your lap for attention and affection. And you stroked him and told him he was a good boy. Of course you did. You wouldn't be human if you didn't. Then, when you were sitting on the sofa and the puppy reached up on his hind legs and put his front paws on you, what did you do? Yup. You know you did what I know you did! And you weren't the only one. The rest of the family did the same, and visitors and members of the public also petted the dog and told you and him how cute he was when he put his paws on their legs for attention.

As the puppy got bigger, you may have tried to stop the behaviour. And how did you do this? Pushed him off? Told him to get off? Looked at him sternly? Acknowledged the behaviour in some other way? Well, by doing any of this you probably inadvertently reinforced/rewarded his jumping up, because he still got the attention he wanted.

There can be several ramifications of your dog jumping up at you or others:

- Embarrassment for you as the behaviour may dirty or rip other people's clothing.

- Concern that a child or elderly person may get hurt.
- Embarrassment that others may feel you are incapable of effective obedience training.

## WHAT'S GOING ON IN THE DOG'S MIND?

We have already discussed what makes dogs do what they do. In the dog's mind, the motivation behind jumping up could be to reunite with you after a period of isolation, as social bonding, or due to the dog's inability to contain his excitement. Sometimes, if a dog is concerned, jumping up and acting the fool can be a displacement behaviour to try to calm a particular situation. Whatever the motivation, the function of the behaviour is to get as close as possible to you and get your attention. The reinforcement for the behaviour is the attention the dog invariably receives, whether that be pushing him off, telling him to get off, or even just looking at him.

## HOW TO RESOLVE THE ISSUE OF JUMPING UP

- Dogs learn by a simple process of repeating behaviour when it is rewarded (inadvertently or otherwise) and not repeating it when there is no reward. Bearing this in mind, the behaviour of jumping up, whether at you or other people, can be addressed using a few tried and tested methods – all of which involve your dog coming to understand that if he jumps up, there will be no reward, but if he offers another behaviour acceptable to us (e.g., all four paws on the floor), there will be a reward in the form of the attention that he so craves. I promise that if you take the specific steps below consistently and regularly, your dog will soon come to realise that it's pointless jumping up at you, Tom, Dick and Harry, and far more rewarding to greet you whilst all four paws are on the floor.

## SPECIFIC ACTIONS FOR JUMPING UP AT YOU

If your dog jumps up, the basic strategy involves you turning your back on him, crossing your arms over your chest and totally ignoring him. If you keep your hands by your side, your dog may be able to reach them and be rewarded without you intending it. This shows your dog that jumping up doesn't bring the reward of attention and affection, so makes the behaviour useless to him – after all, he's doing this with the aim of interacting with you.

• As soon as all four paws are on the ground, you should turn around and praise and calmly pet your dog. If he starts jumping again, repeat the above process. When you do turn round to pet him, bring your hand palm up towards him and stroke him under his chin. This way, if he moves forward to greet your hand, at least all four paws are still on the floor. If you instead go to stroke the top of his head, he may be tempted to lift his front paws to meet your hand. So, make it easy for him by coming from underneath.

## SPECIFIC ACTIONS FOR JUMPING UP AT MEMBERS OF THE PUBLIC – OUTSIDE THE HOME

• Each time you see a member of the public approaching, ask your dog to focus on you and treat him. Hold on to the treat as the person walks by if necessary.

• To have the best chance of success, ask your dog to focus on you before he gets over-aroused by the person coming your way. This might mean asking for his focus when the person is 20 feet away, or 30, or 40. It really does depend on your dog.

• If this strategy is repeated every time whilst on lead, your dog will come to look at you each time someone is walking by because he will come to expect a treat at the sight of people walking by. You will also notice that the distance between your dog and the member of the public, and the distance before you need to distract him, will get smaller and smaller.

• Soon you will be able to get your dog to focus on you even when he is off lead. When practising off lead, extend the distance when directing him to you. Keep in mind the three Ds and the relationship between them. As the challenge of one D is raised, the challenge of the other two Ds needs to be made easier.

• Practise talking to members of the public. Be at the ready. You could redirect your dog when jumping up is imminent or in circumstances when it is known to occur by asking for a mutually exclusive behaviour (e.g., asking your dog to sit), and when he does so, praise him. Alternatively, throw a few treats on the floor. Whilst he's focusing on the treats or sitting as requested, the member of the public may stroke him under his chin. But keep the lead on and ensure he doesn't jump up. If your dog gets too excited by the attention, just take a few steps back.

- Remember, keep your dog on a lead to prevent jumping up and to help in redirecting his attention to you until jumping up has diminished. If your dog jumps up at someone, it's your fault, not the dog's.

- Remember that practise makes perfect. So, don't let your dog practise. Each time he does manage to jump on someone, he is reinforced by the member of public, who is bound to do something other than totally ignore him.

- A long lead could be deployed to prevent jumping up and assist in recall at distances.

- Your kangaroo dog will soon come to understand that jumping up is not wanted; he will also look to you for treats when he sees a member of the public.

- Some behaviourists recommend deployment of a suitable and timely deterrent, whether that be water, sound (a plastic bottle with stones in it, perhaps) or activation of a citronella collar to deter a dog from jumping up. As you know, I advise against such aversive methods and training techniques that are geared only to teach a dog what not to do, rather than teaching the dog the behaviour we would like him to offer instead.

## SPECIFIC ACTIONS FOR JUMPING UP AT VISITORS TO THE HOME

In addition to the strategies set out for members of the public, further strategies are available as follows:

- Teach your dog to go to his bed until he is calm. If he finds this difficult, train him so that he can cope with going to and staying on his bed in the face of visitor distractions. In the short term, you could give him a Kong on his bed with part of his daily portion of food or a chew. Alternatively, use the hook and lead method, as previously discussed.

- Visitors should be told to ignore your dog until he is calm.

- Visitors should be told in advance that if jumping up occurs, they must turn their backs on your dog, cross their arms over their chest and totally ignore him until he has four paws on the ground. Only when his four feet are on the ground should the friend turn around and pet him.

- As with members of the public, you could start off by keeping your dog on a lead when guests arrive or when he is released from his bed. Use the lead to stop him from jumping up. The lead can also be used to help redirect your dog towards food treats thrown on the floor.

- You could also practise sitting with your dog whilst on lead. Ask the visitor to approach. Each time your dog gets overexcited and you think he might try to jump up, the visitor should move away. The visitor should only stroke the dog under his chin (always calmly) if he remains seated or standing with all four paws on the floor.

# CHASING LIGHTS, SHADOWS AND REFLECTIONS

This is a frustrating problem for both dogs and owners. For the dog, it's frustrating because he's never ever going to be able to catch a shadow and this can lead to over-arousal, stress and compulsive behaviours. A dog chasing shadows never seems able to rest and is constantly on the move as soon as he sees even the shadows of passing birds. It can become obsessive, just like other stereotypical behaviours like tail chasing or walking round in circles.

As with all behavioural issues, the way to resolve the problem is by assessing and addressing the root cause. Fortunately, there is an abundance of research on this topic, and several potential reasons have been found for light chasing.

1. **Genetic issues.** This includes the possibility that one of the parent dogs had a compulsive/obsessive personality that has been passed down the line to your dog. Alternatively, your dog may just have a very high prey drive combined with an extremely low threshold for ignoring anything that moves.

2. **Medical issues.** It may be that there are chemical imbalances and the dog is releasing too much dopamine, which drives predatory behaviours. It could be a simple case of a slight defect in hearing that is driving the dog to focus more on visual stimuli. We also know that anxious dogs generally are more prone to react to minor stimuli; anxiety generally tends to exaggerate responses in dogs (and humans). It could also be a nutritional issue, if there is a mineral or vitamin deficiency. If the intensity of the behaviour is the same on each occasion, then that's a sign you might be dealing with a medical issue. If the behaviour is instead caused by external reinforcement, the behaviour is often more intense in different situations. A veterinarian check is always wise with stereotypical behaviours like this, especially if your dog is walking round in circles.

3. **Emotional issues.** Emotional issues can arise from an environment that is lacking in stimulation. Do you remember the six areas of enrichment that are necessary to create a bulletproof dog that we discussed in Chapter 5? In a poorly enriched environment, the poor dog gets totally bored and stressed. Light or tail chasing can become a coping strategy to relieve the stress.

Remember in the olden days, that are sometimes hailed as being golden? Now think about those documentaries that showed gorillas rocking back and forth in their bland zoo enclosures that in no way replicated the environment gorillas need to thrive. Imagine a child in a nursery room with only white walls and devoid of any sensory, visual, auditory and cognitive stimulation. Well, these sorts of environments did exist in orphanages in the 1800s and early 1900s. It was found that the children in these environments were at much greater risk of developing psychiatric disorders and cognitive social-emotional delays. Dogs can suffer the same problems in equally bland environments.

Sometimes, the stress leading to compulsive disorders can arise from major changes in the dog's environment. This could include house renovations or house moves, changes in carers or changes in training methods from positive to aversive techniques.

4. **Learned behaviour.** Several clients confess that they taught the dog to chase a laser light. It was fun initially and provided a good form of exercise. Well, guess what, some breeds such as gun dogs will notice the slightest movement and carry out the predatory motor patterns of chasing and trying to grab the thing that's moving. Motor patterns are maintained by powerful reinforcing chemicals. Each time your dog chases the light, there's a release of hugely reinforcing dopamine. This makes him continue chasing anything that moves, and so the behaviour intensifies. Sometimes, the learned behaviour has taken hold when he's chased a light or shadow and the owner has given the dog generous applause and general attention through laughing. If the dog is seeking your attention and adulation, what better tactic to add to his repertoire?

## HOW TO RESOLVE LIGHT AND SHADOW CHASING

Even more so than with the previous behavioural issues we've covered, it should be clear from the nature of the problem here that the resolution lies more in dealing with the underlying issue causing the problem. If it's medical, sort that out, if possible. Once medical issues have been ruled out, we can start to focus on environmental management, behavioural work as set out below and possibly the use of medication or natural remedies/complementary therapies to help the dog learn whilst we desensitise him to the stimuli. Here's some advice to get you started:

- Remove the lights, reflections and shadows for the moment. This may mean drawing the curtains to cover that part of the opening that is letting in the light. Cover the fridge with the children's art-work if that is letting off reflections. Can we remove shiny reflective toys? Maybe go for walks when it's overcast or at dusk or dawn until desensitisation and any necessary medication has kicked in. One thing you can't do is to ignore the dog's behaviour in the hope that he gets bored with it. He won't. It is likely to get worse and more intense. Sometimes, a distraction and providing something else your dog finds rewarding may suffice, but this does require constant supervision.

- If emotional issues are the root cause of the problem, you will need to focus on meeting your dog's emotional needs. This may involve providing him with a more enriched environment, increased cognitive enrichment and more physical exercise. Remember the three essential needs of a dog that must be met as discussed in Chapter 5: physical needs, emotional needs and mental stimulation, and environmental enrichment needs.

- If the behaviour is rooted in exaggerated reactions and stress caused by anxiety, then the anxiety needs to be dealt with. Stress results in an inability to learn and medical issues. Remember – shouting, ranting and raving will make the anxiety and stress worse and, ergo, the problem worse.

- If your dog breed has predatory motor patterns that have been exaggerated to be sensitive to motion, think about how you can provide appropriate outlets for his self-reinforcing chasing behaviour.

- Use the principle of desensitisation to extinguish the current behavioural response. You will remember from our discussions of desensitisation in Chapter 11, that desensitisation must be done at the dog's pace and not at yours. You will also remember how you will need to reduce the size of the shadow or reflection and then, gradually, increase the challenge for your dog by increasing the size. At the same time, you must reward any behaviour that is an alternative to chasing the light.

# PHOBIAS OF MOTORCYCLES OR LOUD NOISES

Phobias are all about abnormal or irrational fears of something. Most phobias are caused by a traumatic experience (see Chapter 4 for more details). Sometimes the traumatic experience goes unnoticed by the owner, but sometimes a cause can be identified (e.g., a loud lorry driving by or fireworks). Fear-related behaviours can easily become ingrained; your dog barks and the object of his fears (e.g., motorcycle) moves away (it was always going to!) – in your dog's mind, he has been successful and duly rewarded! Sometimes, the anxiety and fear can actually be triggered by the owner feeling anxious and stressed about what the dog might do just before the car goes by or fireworks start.

You will be aware that certain chemicals released in the body and brain lead to emotional responses (if you subscribe to the classical view of emotions). At the very least, the dog's responses will be based on his previous experiences and which coping strategy helped the stress.

## HOW TO RESOLVE PHOBIAS

Depending on the severity of the phobia, medication may be appropriate to help behaviour modification strategies to bed in. In due course, under a veterinarian's guidance, the dog can be weaned off the medication.

In terms of behaviour strategies, we're back to our often-paired heroes: desensitisation and counterconditioning and reinforcement of suitable alternative behaviours.

### First Steps
- Make a recording of the noise made by motorcycles, tractors and any other noise that your dog reacts to or fears.
- Regularly play the different noises to the dog, initially at a low level that does not produce a reaction.
- At the same time, offer treats, feed your dog his daily portions of food, massage him, play a game or whatever else he finds really pleasant.

- At your dog's pace, and this may be after a few minutes, hours or days, the volume can be gradually turned up. Continue with feeding, playing a game or treating.

- Do not reassure or pat your dog if he shows any reaction to the noise. Instead, calmly ignore and reduce the noise level – you are moving too fast for him.

- You must stay calm and assertive at all times.

- Do the above with a visual recording played on the TV of motorcycles, tractors, cyclists, etc. YouTube is a good source for this type of material.

- Once comfortable with noises and visuals on TV, ask a friend to park his motorcycle on your drive and allow your dog to become accustomed to it. If it's tractors that your dog has a problem with, well, find a stationary one and be near enough to it that it doesn't bother your dog. Unless, of course, you have friends with tractors, in which case, lucky you!

- Once your dog is accustomed to the motorcycle, the ante can be raised by running the motorcycle whilst your dog is watching at a comfortable distance. If he shows no reaction, he should be rewarded.

### Next Steps

- When your dog has become totally accustomed to the noise and visuals on TV and in the flesh, find an appropriate place, e.g., a busy road, and confront the object of his fears, always at a distance he can tolerate. Then use the same strategy for dogs that are aggressive towards people.

- Let your dog see the source of his fear at a threshold distance (outside his worry zone and in his safe zone) where he is calm and shows no nervous behaviour. When he looks at the target, mark that behaviour by telling him 'good boy' or 'yes' and give him a treat. Practise, practise, practise. In due time, you won't even have to mark the behaviour. Your dog will see the source of his fears and, expecting a treat, look at you. So, treat him. This is exactly what we want. When he sees a motorcycle, he looks at you rather than barking or lunging. In this way, your dog will learn that the things he feared are an environmental cue that good things will happen. At the same time, he is also learning the alternative behaviour that you want him to do (since that is being rewarded). Soon, the alternative rewarded behaviour becomes the default behaviour.

- As an alternative, once your dog has seen the source of his fears, by voice you can redirect his attention and encourage him to keep his focus on you (e.g., through asking for a sit or 'watch me'). Every time he ignores the source of his fears and looks to you or otherwise complies with your request, he should be rewarded with treats or a toy/game.
- Vary the place and time of the exercise.
- Gradually reduce the distance between the dog and the source of his fears, and continue to reward.
- Always finish the training session on a positive.

For the best chance of success, ensure slow introduction over many weeks and many times a week. Don't force your dog to go too fast or shout or threaten him if he becomes frightened. A reaction from your dog simply means that you are moving too fast for him. Instead, calmly move to a distance at which your dog is comfortable. It can sometimes help to reassure your dog and speed up the rehabilitation of the phobia of loud noises if he is accompanied by a calm and confident dog.

# PREY DRIVE - CHASING CARS, CYCLISTS

Has your dog ever chased and bitten a cyclist? If he has, the incident would obviously be a major cause for concern and extremely distressing for you. The cyclist was probably also not very happy.

There are four main reasons why dogs chase runners, cyclists and other moving targets. For this section, let's discard territorial chasing. That would only be a consideration if the behaviour happened whilst your dog was on home ground. Let's also discard chasing for the purpose of socialising. That doesn't normally result in a bite at the end.

This leaves chasing motivated by fear or chasing due to innate predatory motor patterns.

When a dog is aggressive because of **fear**, the purpose of any aggression and chasing (see Chapter 1) is to increase the distance between the dog and the source of his fears. Fear, originating from a traumatic experience, can lead to stress and consequent aggression when faced with a similar situation. Fear and anxiety around runners and cyclists may also have originated from a dog simply not having been adequately socialised or habituated to these stimuli, particularly during puppyhood. As we covered in Chapter 11, resolving fear in dogs normally involves behaviour modification through a process of desensitisation and counterconditioning. But for the purposes of this section, let's say that the chasing on this occasion is not rooted in fear.

Sometimes, the root cause of chasing behaviours can be due to **predatory motor pattern instincts to chase fast-moving objects.** This could be animals but could also extend to runners and cyclists. The purpose of the dog's prey drive is to decrease distance between the dog and the thing he is chasing.

## WHAT'S GOING ON IN THE DOG'S MIND?

The prey drive is an instinctive behaviour and hugely rewarding for the dog. Aspects of the prey drive pattern have often been emphasised through selective breeding. For example, the grab-bite element of the basic motor pattern, eye > stalk > chase > grab-bite > kill-bite > dissect > consume, has been emphasised for Australian cattle dogs. The kill-bite element of the basic motor pattern has been emphasised for terriers, traditionally used to kill rats.

If your dog is a mix of breeds, he may have inherited a high prey drive. If so, he may be driven by chemicals to carry out his predatory behaviour. These chemicals boost feelings of pleasure. Dogs with a high prey drive are constantly looking for outlets to practise the behaviour. If your dog has low levels of impulse control, that is likely to exacerbate his high prey drive.

Instinctive behaviours like the prey drive are hard to stop as they can't be totally removed. This is because the chase will always be hugely rewarding for the dog due to the release of excitatory chemicals (dopamine and adrenaline). These chemicals make it very difficult for a dog to exercise the impulse control he might show under normal circumstances. A piece of chicken and even a reliable recall is simply not going to work once your dog is absorbed in the chase.

## HOW TO HELP KEEP THE DOG OUT OF TROUBLE CAUSED BY A HIGH PREY DRIVE

Whilst a dog's prey drive cannot be totally removed, it can be curbed or reduced. Three principal changes need to be made for a successful outcome:

1. **Change the relationship between the owner and the dog.** This involves forging a stronger connection so the dog is more likely to listen to his owner.

2. **Change the relationship between the dog and the 'prey'.** The dog needs to understand that, for example, sheep are verboten.

3. **Change the dog's general environment to ensure unnecessary stresses are removed.** Chasing makes a dog feel good. If a dog is already in a happy place, he is less likely to chase to seek relief from his stress to make him feel better. Be mindful of the things that your dog might find stressful:

- Pain somewhere in his body
- Illness
- Digestive issues
- Slippery floors at home
- Not enough sleep
- Not enough outlets for his prey drive

- Punishment-based training methods
- Too much human traffic

In addition to removing as much stress as possible, don't forget to increase activities that make your dog feel better. Finally, ensuring that the three essential needs of your dog (physical, emotional and mental stimulation) are met is essential.

The four main positive, reward-based strategies for controlling prey drive are: **prevention of an inappropriate chase through environmental management, improving your dog's impulse control, providing alternative safer prey drive opportunities and activities** and finally, **habituation.**

# PREVENTION

Whether the motivation for the chase is born of fear, prey drive or an element of both, the following is vital:

- You must maintain an awareness of the environment to ensure there is no repeat of the chase behaviour. If you notice something that is likely to result in a chase, get your dog on a short, six-foot lead. This must be done until the strategies for curbing his prey drive through impulse control training have had an impact and there have been no incidents of chasing in the presence of a cyclist for, say, two whole months.
- When you do eventually allow your dog off a short lead, it must be under strictly controlled circumstances, including the use of a long line. The aim is always to control your dog's impulse to chase prior to any chase commencing.

Prolonged prevention in the face of constant exposure to runners and cyclists should see a gradual decline in the dog's chase instincts.

# IMPULSE CONTROL TRAINING

There are several ways your dog's impulse control can be improved. However, training must be practised every day to overcome the problem/decrease the chances of the predatory motor patterns recurring.

# GENERAL ADVICE FOR IMPULSE CONTROL

- Engage your dog and teach him new desirable behaviours such as waiting when a door is opened rather than rushing through, and being calm around food, which can be practised using various techniques.

- Teaching 'stay' and 'watch me'. Every opportunity should be taken to practise and perfect these cues. 'Stay' or 'hold', for example, could be practiced when throwing a ball, a toy, a piece of food or when using a flirt pole.

# REINFORCEMENT OF ALTERNATIVE BEHAVIOURS

This involves handsomely rewarding your dog immediately and consistently when he complies with an instruction to focus on you or to 'stay' or 'hold'. Of course, if he looks at something he wants to chase and instead offers any behaviour other than chasing, reward that too! Practise this whenever you happen to come across a cyclist or runner.

Should your dog start to eye a cyclist/runner, you could ask him to 'watch me'. If he stops the intense eye focus, he can then be rewarded. At that stage, you can ask for another behaviour that is incompatible with chasing, such as a 'sit', then reward him again. If the intensity of his focus does not diminish, you're likely far too close to the cyclist/runner, so calmly increase the distance.

But, three things to remember. First, you must work with the target of the chase outside the zone in which your dog reacts. Secondly, you must let him see the thing he wants to chase before you reward him for an alternative behaviour, whether you requested it or not. Thirdly, don't be mean with the treats. Work with uber-high favourite treats.

This strategy in the face of constant exposure to runners and cyclists should see a gradual decline in your dog's default position of chasing.

# PREDICTIVE REDIRECTION

There's lots of different ways you can teach your dog that whenever he sees a runner or cyclist, he needs to look somewhere else and that looking somewhere else means something great happens. We've already discussed one way in the section dealing with dogs being aggressive towards members of the public.

A lovely game you can practise was suggested by David Ryan and, with his permission, I've set it out verbatim below under his coined title 'Predictive Redirection'. Basically, the game involves redirecting your dog's chase behaviour onto a specific toy or game. The game could involve a ball, be a game of tug or anything that your dog finds sufficiently alluring to take his mind off the runner/cyclist. To make this strategy work, it is vital that:

- The toy or game should only be used during training.
- It should be ingrained into your dog's mind that when a predictive word (e.g., 'toy') is used, it consistently involves the presentation of the game or toy.
- You need to teach your dog to focus on the toy or game in low-distraction environments first. The predictive redirection must be 100% secure, 100% of the time, for at least a month prior to testing with distant (and eventually at a lesser distance), known, volunteer runners and cyclists, in a variety of environments.

## *PREDICTIVE REDIRECTION* by David Ryan[23]

*(Initially, practice in a place with no distractions)*

*1. Call, "Toy!" or "Ball!" in a bright and breezy voice every time you throw the toy for your dog. Soon, he will associate the word with the unconditional arrival of the toy/commencement of a game.*

*2. Start to use the word when he is not expecting it. Call, "Ball!" and as soon as he looks, throw it behind you. The word becomes* **predictive** *that there is a game on offer. Once he is reliably engaged with the toy, you should proceed to the next steps.*

*3. Take two identical favourite toys and ask your dog to "sit"/"stay" while you throw the first one as far as you can without using the "Ball!" command. If he won't sit/stay, keep him on a lead or hold his collar.*

*4. Then call "Ball!" and throw the second toy. He will have forgotten about the first toy.*

*5. Then repeat step 3 and wait for a count of five, then give a "fetch" command and release your dog. Immediately call, "Ball!"*

---

23      Ryan, D. (2009) 'How do I stop my dog chasing?' *David Ryan: Dog Behaviour Author.* Available from https://www.dog-secrets.co.uk/how-do-i-stop-my-dog-chasing/

and throw the second toy past his nose. As the first toy is dead and the second still moving, he will choose the 'live' toy to chase.

6. Then pick up the 'dead' one, ask for the 'live' one back and repeat.

If your dog doesn't stop for the 'live' toy but pursues the 'dead' one, substitute the first thing you throw for something less valuable, to make it less attractive. Don't worry if he goes searching for the 'dead' one after he's picked up the 'live' one, you have achieved your goal by focussing him on the second toy.

• After three or four throws, your dog may not set off after the first one, but wait for you to call, "Ball!". Don't reward that with the second toy, but send him on – going with him to find and play with the first one if necessary. You control the game; don't be manipulated by your dog.

• Start again. This time wait until he is a third of the way to the first one before calling "Ball!" and throwing the second toy.

• Next time call, "Ball!" but don't throw the second one immediately. Wave it above your head for him to see and, when he starts to come back, reward him with the throw.

• Leave it later and later to call your dog back and then start to reduce the time the first toy is 'dead' before calling "Ball!" and sending him for the second toy.

• Your final aim is to throw the first toy, immediately send him, wait until he is almost there, call, "Ball!" and wait until he comes all the way back to you, before playing with/ throwing the second one. It'll take a little time to achieve, but this is an excellent exercise to curb the chase instinct.

**Once the distraction is secure it is time to practice with a <u>volunteer</u> runner/cyclist.**

**Step 1** – Put your dog on a long, slack leash and stand at least 3 metres behind him.

**Step 2** – Create a controlled environment which is likely to make him chase a runner. Instruct the volunteer to run past your dog – initially at some distance.

**Step 3** – Monitor your dog's behaviour and gestures. Wait until he gives a sign that he's about to start the chase, e.g., an intense focus.

**Step 4** – Issue the "Ball!" command. Time the command – ensure he hears it before he begins to chase.

*Step 5 – If your dog comes straight away, you should issue lots of verbal praise. If he ignores you, you're moving too fast for your dog and you need to go back to previous steps and ingrain those. Alternatively, reduce the size of the runner, by increasing distance.*

*Step 6 – Repeat the exercise for 20 minutes a day until you are confident that your dog will respond to the predictive redirection.*

*Step 7 – Once you are confident, practice the exercise without the leash but with a muzzle – it won't overly matter if your dog can't pick up the ball whilst muzzled. Alternatively, you may proceed directly to Step 8 below.*

*Step 8 – Should you be in total control of your dog and no chase has been given for several months, you may be tempted to practice with volunteers without a muzzle. Should your dog ignore the predictive redirection whilst off leash and without a muzzle, the volunteer should stop running, throw food towards your dog and stay motionless to avoid him proceeding to the grab-bite of the motor pattern sequence.*

*Step 9 - Ultimately, you may be tempted to progress to your dog being off leash and un-muzzled in public.*

***However, as I have mentioned earlier, this could be a costly mistake. In my view, if your dog has a bite history, it would be safer for your dog to always remain muzzled whilst off leash in public.***

## RECALL

If predictive redirection doesn't work for you, perfect your recall in the usual fashion, as discussed in Chapter 7.

To avoid all associations with previous failed attempts, it may be appropriate to start from fresh and re-start training using a whistle. Try approaching the training in the following way:

- Condition your dog to the whistle, i.e., each time the whistle is blown, it must be followed by a treat.
- Five sessions per day for three days; each session should be about two or three minutes. This should be practised at close quarters. High value treats should be on offer (sausage?). The whistle must be blown in the same way on each occasion. On each occasion the treat is given, the collar should be touched or the neck should be stroked.
- Repeat, but add a short distance (on 6ft lead). The dog should come to you. If he doesn't, use the lead and take a step back.

- Repeat blowing the whistle randomly in the home.
- Practise with a longer lead attached first, and then, without.
- Repeat in the garden. Start with short distances, then increase to longer distances on a long lead.
- Repeat outside in the park with no distractions, then with low level distractions on a long lead.
- Repeat without a long lead at short distances, increasing to long distances. Start with no distractions, and move to increased distractions.

## PROVIDING ALTERNATIVE SAFER PREY DRIVE OPPORTUNITIES

Alternate opportunities for the dog to use his prey drive should be provided in a secure and controlled environment without runners or cyclists. These safer opportunities will reinforce your dog for performing his innate behaviour in a controlled arena. Consequently, he'll be less inclined to find his own outlet in chasing runners/cyclists. In addition to the predictive redirection activity described above, such activities might include:

- Frisbee or ball play – this could be in your garden or a hired field.
- Sheepdog training, Treibball and other courses and classes.
- Use of a flirt pole.
- Hide and seek.

In addition, Simone Mueller, author of *Hunting Together: Harnessing Predatory Chasing in Family Dogs through Motivation-Based Training*, considers allowing your dog to carry out the 'safe parts' of his predatory motor pattern as a useful way forward. This way, the dog can still gain the pleasure of practising aspects of predation rather than preventing a natural behaviour completely.

## HABITUATION

When other animals are not introduced to dogs appropriately or appropriate socialisation has not taken place during the dog's sensitive period (the first 5 to 12 weeks of a puppy's life), the consequences can be disastrous. It's useful to apply the concept of introducing dogs to other animals when dealing with chasing behaviour. Advice on this can be found in Chapter 10.

If there have been no incidents of chasing on a long lead for several months, you might at some stage consider it safe to unleash your dog in a public place. However, especially if your dog has a bite history, even though he may remain incident free for several months, there is always a danger that, given a perfect storm, he may give chase and inflict a bite. Because of this, my advice is that when off leash in public, **dogs with this sort of problem should always be muzzled.** This will prevent a further biting episode in the event of a chase during a lapse in your attention. This is not only a responsible way forward, but if your dog does bite again, you could be held liable under the Animals Act 1971.

# BARKING

In Chapter 8, we covered dog language and how barking is one way for dogs and many other species to communicate their needs. It's a natural behaviour, and discouraging a dog from expressing and sharing his feelings would be inappropriate and disempowering. Yet, people attempt to do so through various methods:

- Spraying a barking dog with water or shouting.
- Undertaking a controversial debarking surgery.
- The use of various 'Stop Barking' products that are freely available on the market and touted as resolving barking issues.
- The use of shock collars, which are still legal and used is some countries.

The vast majority, if not all, of these methods fail for one important reason. They do not address the initial motivation for the dog barking. Furthermore, many of the strategies mentioned above risk the development of other behavioural problems.

It follows that when dealing with barking issues, it is not the barking itself that necessarily needs to be addressed, but the cause of the barking. So, by way of a reminder, let's look at some of the main reasons why dogs may bark, potentially excessively.

1. Separation-related disorders.
2. Medical reasons.
3. Being alarmed when outside the home.
4. Fear.
5. Guarding of territory or people.
6. As a form of seeking attention, perhaps through boredom or loneliness.
7. As a form of greeting and during play.

In summary, barking can be due to medical reasons, an expression of emotion or feeling, or because the act of barking has previously been rewarded.

## HOW TO DEAL WITH EXCESSIVE BARKING

On the basis that we generally need to address the cause to deal with the manifestation (barking), the starting point is to ascertain that cause. In brief, if the barking is due to any one of the reasons listed in 1–5 above, we need to address the cause. If the barking is a form of attention seeking or greeting, we will need to stop rewarding the barking and start rewarding alternative and more acceptable behaviours.

## SEPARATION ANXIETY/MEDICAL REASONS

How to deal with separation disorders has already been covered under the 'Separation Anxiety' section of this chapter, starting at p. 125. Essentially, the only way to resolve barking due to separation anxiety is to resolve the anxiety.

If your dog's compulsive barking is instead due to medical reasons (for example, a canine cognitive disorder or other brain disorders), a veterinarian will need to be involved to identify and resolve the root cause, often with the help of medication. Medication can help the dog learn and adopt more acceptable behaviours.

## ALARM/FEAR BARKING

With this type of barking, we need to deal with the stimulus that is causing the fear that leads to the barking. This is where desensitisation and counterconditioning come into play, as discussed in Chapter 11.

## TERRITORIAL BARKING

It's worth mentioning that when a dog barks whenever someone approaches the front door, he is often motivated by fear. In those circumstances, desensitisation and counterconditioning is useful in modifying the barking behaviour. In addition, teaching the dog to be quiet and then rewarding him when he stops barking is a good strategy for controlling excessive barking.

Teaching the dog to stop barking can be straightforward. The way to do this is to say 'quiet' in a calm, firm voice when your dog is barking. Put your hand up in front of him as a policeman might when stopping traffic. As soon as he stops barking, reward him with something extra tasty. Your dog should soon work out that when he stops barking, there's a huge reward for him.

Territorial guarding (including guarding people) is often heightened in guarding breeds, such as Dobermans and German shepherd dogs. These dogs should not be encouraged to guard in the first instance. The barking can be reduced by managing the environment. Limiting the visual stimuli of people going by the door, drawing curtains, placing the dog in a back room and so on can all help.

## ATTENTION-SEEKING BARKING

Many behaviours continue because of exogenous (as opposed to endogenous) reinforcement. Dogs often jump up at us with the motivation of seeking attention. This jumping up is rewarded when we provide the dog with the attention so craved by instinctively touching, talking or looking at the jumping dog.

The pupil dog so quickly becomes the teacher and you, the teacher, so quickly can become the pupil. I certainly feel this with Frank. I teach him to look at me and when he does, I reward him. Knowing that he gets a reward when he looks at me, he now regularly looks at me when he wants a treat. I oblige. Oh dear. I've become the pupil here and Frank, the teacher.

The story is the same with barking. When Frank wants toast, he lets out a funny little bark. My wife finds this amusing and importantly, gives him a piece of toast. I ignore Frank when he barks at me for toast. Consequently, he barks at my wife more frequently, but rarely at me. Instead, he calmly goes to his bed. He is then rewarded by me with a piece of toast.

In short, ignoring unwanted barking that has been previously rewarded and rewarding alternative behaviours, such as not barking, sitting or going to his bed, should soon reduce or eliminate the excessive barking. For optimum results on rewarding alternative behaviours, reward once the dog has been quiet or has displayed the alternative behaviour for four seconds or so – especially when dealing with attention seeking and greeting rituals towards people.

It is important, however, to first rule out barking due to boredom or loneliness. Always ensure that your dog's three essential needs (physical, emotional, and cognitive and environmental enrichment) are met.

## GREETING/PLAY BARKING

This is often displayed by dogs going into a frenzy of barking or boisterous leaping around when you first come downstairs in the morning or when you return home from work. Barking in these circumstances is again more likely to be due to such behaviour having been previously rewarded. To counter this behaviour (or other similar boisterous behaviour), the best course of action is to ignore your dog and then instantly reward him when he's quiet. Alternatively, you could ask for a substitute behaviour to the barking (e.g., 'bed' or 'sit'), and then reward him as soon as he offers the behaviour requested.

# RESOLVING MULTIPLE PROBLEMS

We've covered a number of specific behavioural issues that you may have experienced with your current or previous dog. However, dogs rarely display only one behavioural concern with one underlying cause. Often, there are numerous underlying factors that contribute to the particular behavioural concern, and usually, I'm instructed where a dog is displaying a number of behaviours the client would like modified. In these types of cases, an early assessment needs to be made on what area to tackle first, or whether it is one or two main factors that are causing and linked to all the behavioural concerns. In the latter case, a holistic approach might be more appropriate.

So, having read this book, let's check your knowledge and see how you would cope if you were presented with some behavioural concerns. Here are the brief facts of a case I came across. What is your view? Once you've had a go, have a look at my thoughts on p. 194.

*Billy is a cockapoo aged seven. He shares the home with a four-year-old, boisterous German shepherd called Rex.*

*Billy is a bit anxious and prone to aggression if he gets scared. He has bitten the owners when they try to cut his nails. He's also bitten the owners when they have tried to move him from the kitchen.*

*Billy also destroys the kitchen sofa when left alone, but only in the winter months.*

*Billy is on supplements and medication for his arthritis and has skin sensitivities and is allergic to poultry.*

With these facts being the only facts at your disposal:

- **Why does Billy destroy the sofa when left alone in the winter months?**
- **Why is Billy biting his owners when they try and move him from the kitchen?**
- **Why is Billy biting his owners when they try to cut his nails?**
- **What should the owners do to prevent being bitten and help Billy's anxiety?**

This is not a straightforward case, and before venturing a response, here's some further information I would want to know if you had instructed me on this:

- A list of all stimuli/triggers that scare Billy and trigger his nervousness and biting.
- Distance of triggers, or noise levels, or intensity of smells before there is a reaction and over-reaction from Billy.
- What is Rex doing when Billy is reacting or over-reacting?
- What signals does Billy give off before he bites?
- Have there been any changes in Billy's diet or the environment or the relationship between the owners prior to the behavioural issues starting?
- Are the owners in agreement over the issues and the outcomes required?
- Is there anything unsafe on the countryside walks Billy is taken on, e.g., poisonous plants?
- Other than climatic changes between October and January, have the owners noticed any other changes in the winter, e.g., firework noises, gunshots?
- The weather conditions when Billy does become destructive, e.g., rain, thunder, lightning, low/high pressure systems.
- Where precisely does Billy seek safety when he runs away? When did he first start seeking out this safe place?
- Does Rex's boisterous behaviour impact Billy?
- Has Rex ever hurt Billy, accidentally or otherwise?
- Is Billy ever 'aggressive' towards Rex?
- Dates of the bite incidents, and the precise conditions immediately prior to the bites. What precisely did the owners do after the bites, and what did Billy do after each bite?
- Have the owners used anything other than positive reinforcement to get Billy to do what they wanted? If so, what did the owners do, and how does Billy react to the owners' actions?
- Dates for the onset of pain and mobility issues and initial prescription of pain relieving and mobility medication.
- Any incidents or accidents with nail clippers and grooming brush.
- Do the owners always groom in the same place/room/times?
- What noises emanate from the outside environment that Billy can hear, and are these loud noises or constant noises?

- Has Billy's behaviour changed since starting his medication?
- Does Billy have any other medical issues that might impact on the behaviours presented (e.g., noise sensitivity, any endocrine or neurological disorders)?
- Does Billy have any teeth problems?
- Is there a rodent infestation?
- Does the sofa destruction only occur when Billy is left alone, or is Rex involved/present?
- Do the owners have time constraints on implementing behaviour modification strategies and training generally?
- General ability of owners to implement behaviour modification strategies and their level of general dog knowledge, including body language relating to warning signals.
- Is Billy crate trained/can he easily be crate trained?
- What mental enrichment activities do the owners currently undertake with Billy that provide him with opportunities to use his brain, and does this and the general physical activity of the owners with Billy decrease during the winter?
- Have the behaviours got worse, or have they remained the same in terms of severity or speed of reaction?
- Were Billy's parents of a nervous disposition?

Now here are my views on the specific questions:

## WHY DOES BILLY DESTROY THE SOFA WHEN LEFT ALONE IN THE WINTER MONTHS?

There could be several reasons for Billy's destructive behaviours being worse in winter.

- Billy may be reacting due to a sensitivity to or phobia of noises in the environment which are more prevalent during these seasons, including fireworks around 5th November, Diwali and New Year.
- Billy may be reacting to climatic noise changes including rain, increased wind speeds, or thunder. Some of these noises may have become conditioned stimuli, resulting in a conditioned anxiety/fear response through classical conditioning.
- Billy may be able to sense the arrival of bad weather through changes in barometric pressure changes. If Billy is fearful of bad

weather, these barometric pressure changes are likely to make him anxious.

- Research suggests that reduced daylight may cause seasonal affective disorder (SAD) and therefore a downturn in Billy's mood.

- Lack of exercise and stimulation can cause boredom, leading a dog to find outlets, which can often result in destructive and other antisocial behaviours. This could be the result of the owners themselves not being keen on winter weather and therefore going on fewer walks and being less active with Billy.

- The shooting season of pheasants and partridges occurs between September and February. Due to the location of Billy's residence, this may be causing him distress and lead to him displaying destructive behaviours during this period.

- The triggers in the environment such as noises may be causing Billy to become anxious or fearful, causing activation of the sympathetic nervous system and stress response. Billy is likely to try to alleviate this stress by doing whatever is best for him in the situation. Chewing is soothing and calming for dogs as it releases endogenous opioids. Biting and tearing at the sofas may also release tension. Separation anxiety may also be a factor in activating the panic/grief system. Separation in mammals can lead to homeostasis changes, corticosterone secretion, negative valence and arousal leading to 'behavioural reactivity'. This reactivity could result in Billy damaging the sofa. Additionally, there may be an element of boredom leading to antisocial behaviours – as mentioned above – that Billy is trying to alleviate through chewing on and destroying the sofa.

- If it is specifically Billy that is destroying the sofa, rather than Rex or both dogs, it may be that the random exposure to noise when he is left alone has conditioned Billy to become fearful. When he is left outside of his safe area, this is likely to cause Billy to become more fearful, frustrated and anxious, and to panic when noises occur.

## WHY IS BILLY BITING HIS OWNERS WHEN THEY TRY AND MOVE HIM FROM THE KITCHEN?

This is likely due to frustration because Billy is unable to employ coping strategies in dealing with his fear or anxiety in response to triggers in the environment. An anxious dog is emotionally reactive because he perceives a threat or perhaps because he has felt threatened on a previous occasion in similar circumstances. Alternatively, a novel situation can cause anxiety. Fear eventually turns into frustration if a dog is prevented from carrying out a behaviour. That frustration can then very quickly turn into rage. This link between fear and frustration is supported by research.

Another way of looking at this is that Billy becomes anxious because he comes to predict that scary things are going to happen (the noises) when the owners remove him from the kitchen. Furthermore, removing his control over the environment by denying him his safe place/haven also makes him anxious. The direct confrontation by the owners is seen as a threat by Billy. Since Billy is also denied an escape option, he has no alternative but to either bite or cower and shut down. Billy chooses the former.

## WHY IS BILLY BITING HIS OWNERS WHEN THEY TRY TO CUT HIS NAILS?

Billy is on several medications to relieve pain and mobility. This suggests joint pain, which could be due to an injury or arthritis. Physiological pain could be a cause of the aggression as Billy tries to avoid it. It may be that this pain is exacerbated due to pressure on the joints or bending his legs to get access to allow nail clipping. It may also be due to chronic pain, leading to hyperalgesia or allodynia, an increased reaction to pain.

Alternatively, Billy may be frightened because he has not been habituated to having his nails clipped. He may also be anxious or fear having his nails clipped due to a past traumatic experience of pain, e.g., having had his quick cut. If this is the case, the aggressive behaviour is most likely linked to the fear, and the function of the behaviour is likely to be to increase distance. Having succeeded in getting the owners to back off after a previous display of aggression, the neurochemical reinforcement of dopamine predicts that the owners will back off again, and Billy's behaviour will thereby be reinforced. The history of the owners backing off after being bitten will have reinforced Billy to repeat the behaviour.

## WHAT SHOULD THE OWNERS DO TO

# PREVENT BEING BITTEN AND HELP BILLY'S ANXIETY?

First, they should improve Billy's daily life by:

- Ensuring any pain due to arthritis is as low as possible. A veterinarian must advise on this and the potential use of appropriate medication. The vet may also suggest supplements (such as green-lipped muscle, hyaluronic acid (found in Yumove Plus), Bromelain, Pycnogenol, vitamin $D_3$) and a good quality food that contains glucosamine, MSM and chondroitin.

- Alleviating as much unnecessary stress as possible from Billy's life. Chronic stress can cause dishabituation (causing a dog to react to a stimulus to which he had previously habituated) and could cause Billy's inflammatory condition to worsen. Chronic stress involves high circulating glucocorticoid levels, which can also dysregulate the HPA axis feedback. This can affect the hippocampus and amygdala – connected to learning and memory – and cause decreased activation in the pre-frontal cortex, potentially leading to permanent damage to memory function. Chronic stress can also cause a number of medical issues and a decline in a dog's mental and physical welfare.

- It would be helpful to create a calming environment for Billy, potentially with the help of prescription and complementary therapies such as pheromones, Bach flower remedies, wraps, etc. In the meantime, desensitisation work around stressors to build Billy's resilience to them would help.

- In addition to reducing stressors in Billy's life, as well as building up Billy's resilience, and as requested by the owners, activities in Billy's daily life should include opportunities for enrichment by utilising the play system and the lower end of the seeking system, thereby increasing serotonin and dopamine levels that will put him in a good mood. These activities shouldn't exacerbate his medical condition. This should include breed specific activities, e.g., hunting, swimming, retrieving and searching, that are all part of Billy's predatory motor pattern.

- Food should be presented in such a way as to maximise mental stimulation. Scatter feeding, for example, will give Billy the opportunity to use his nose, which he will find intrinsically rewarding. Each time Billy looks for a piece of kibble, dopamine will be released. However, variety in the way food or other activities that engage the lower ends of the seeking system are provided is important, as the seeking system, once habituated, produces less dopamine. Dopamine is, of course, a crucial element in learning. The mental stimulation will be vital in alleviating Billy's boredom and any consequential destructive behaviours.

Secondly, whilst implementing strategies to remove stress from Billy's life, the owners should in the meantime manage the environment so that Billy is unable to practise destructive behaviours. This could be done by moving the sofa out of the safe room rather than moving Billy out of the safe room and preventing him from employing any coping strategy. Instead of the sofa, a safer alternative could be left in the room for Billy to destroy until desensitisation work around noises had been successful. In addition, Rex could be left in another room in case he is exacerbating Billy's stress. They could be separated by way of a baby gate.

In addition, work needs to be done to condition Billy to a soft, comfortable mat in his safe area. This should be made into Billy's safety signal. This can be done by pairing it with low level noise and great things happening on the mat through the use of treats, massages or whatever else rocks Billy's boat. This is all about desensitisation and counterconditioning, two principles we have discussed previously.

Thirdly, having removed, reduced or resolved (through desensitisation principles) the overreaction to potential triggers, there are two specific areas that may be causing Billy stress, which need to be addressed as follows:

• Resolve the separation related disorder. Billy's destructive behaviour, repetitive behaviours and pacing when the owners are absent are indicators that a separation disorder exists and the activation of the panic/grief system. We've already looked at this. The owner's presence reduces distress through release of neuropeptides, including endogenous opioids, oxytocin and prolactin.

• Billy biting the owners. Currently, he sees the owners as aversive, as moving him may be associated with potential pain due to arthritis. Furthermore, the tension associated with being moved from a safe place may also exacerbate the pain that Billy feels. This is likely to lead to anxiety, with the possible activation of the fear circuitry, as previously discussed in Chapter 3. This means Billy will wish to avoid the consequent negative affect. Due to the huge internal neurochemical reinforcement in the form of dopamine, Billy's behaviour of biting is likely to continue and escalate.

If moving Billy is required at any stage, all direct confrontation between Billy and his owners should cease immediately. Moving Billy should be done through positive reinforcement. That is likely to increase his compliance. Furthermore, moving him in a safe way means Billy is unable to practise the biting behaviour. Perhaps he could be placed on a lead to prompt him to a different position using positive reinforcement.

Grooming and nail clipping is also causing Billy to bite the owners. This should stop until the reason for this behaviour has been addressed and resolved. Is it pain? If so, allow the medication to kick in. If it is through fear or anxiety because of a previous traumatic event, then desensitising and counterconditioning in relation to grooming should be done. Alternatively, change the picture in Billy's mind about what grooming looks like. Start from scratch in such a way that Billy doesn't even know that grooming training has started.

Start this new training in a different room/area to where it has been carried out before to avoid any negative associations with the previous triggers and environments. Rather than nail clippers, use nail grinders. Rather than grooming him standing up, start with him lying down. Remember to break up the grooming routine into small steps and small approximations (see Chapter 6 for training tips). Finally, train Billy in some behaviours that will help in the grooming process, for example, a calm settle, a chin rest (as shown by Pat Koven – a licensed veterinary technician with over 25 years' experience), teach Billy the names of body parts as cues that they will be touched (e.g., 'paw', touch), treat. There's also a fantastic game first mentioned by Chirag Patel called the 'Bucket Game' that can help with this. A search on YouTube throws up a number of helpful videos on teaching you how to get your dog used to grooming.

How did you do? Did you manage to get most of the points? If so, holy brainbox, Batman! Very knowledgeable – go to the top of the class!

# FINAL WORD

I've been very fortunate over the years to have worked with most types of dog breeds. I've also been fortunate in having worked with most types of clients, ranging from the very knowledgeable to novices. From each dog and each client I have learned something new, and they have learned something new from me. But there is one constant that has remained. In the vast majority of cases, the dogs are simply doing what is normal to meet their needs in the circumstances. The behaviour is not the problem; behaviour tells me that there is a problem. It's not the 'behaviour' that needs addressing but the cause of the behaviour. What clients actually want, though they don't know it, is for the dog to show a different behaviour to the one that the dog normally offers.

The focus of this book has been to arm owners with a greater understanding, more compassion and a thirst to gain even more knowledge and better the lives of their dogs. The book helps owners understand why the dog is offering behaviours the owner finds egregious and teaches them how to use kind and positive reinforcement methods to persuade their dog to carry out alternative behaviours that they like and that equally meet the dog's needs. This has a beneficial knock-on effect, which is the true aim of the book – dogs and owners living in harmony.

# QUIZ ANSWERS

**1. Play-biting among puppies and in relation to humans:**
- Is an unnatural behaviour that is unacceptable.
- **Is a natural behaviour that helps to establish bite inhibition – a sense of how hard they can bite without causing injury.**
- Always stops of its own accord as the dog matures.
- Should be encouraged to develop a strong character.

**2. The main cause of separation anxiety is:**
- **When a puppy/dog gets excessive attention or has not been conditioned to an appropriate routine.**
- Breed predisposition.
- Lack of obedience training.
- The house in which the dog resides being too big.

**3. What are the three main reasons for destructive behaviour?**
- Attention seeking, fun and exercise.
- Breed predisposition, over-excitement and exercise.
- **Normal puppy behaviour, boredom and separation anxiety.**
- Resentment, onset of gum disease and monotony.

**4. If your dog is whining because of separation anxiety, you should:**
- Ignore him.
- Reprimand him and then praise him when he's quiet.
- **Help him understand that there's nothing to be anxious about.**
- Put some calming music on to distract him.

**5. If your dog stops to say hello to another dog when you're training him to walk to heel, you should:**
- Stop when the dog stops, thereby keeping the leash loose.
- Stop, as otherwise you are preventing the dog from exploring.
- Reprimand the dog as a demonstration of your leadership.
- **Continue walking.**

**6. It is recommended that you do not allow a puppy to lick people's faces because:**
- It is a serious risk to human health.
- It is established that this can lead to obsessive-compulsive behaviours.
- It may cause separation related problems.
- **It may encourage jumping up as the dog matures.**

**7. When a dog solicits attention from you through pawing, jumping up and such like, you should NOT:**
- Ignore the dog by avoiding eye contact, touch and voice acknowledgement.
- Stand up to prevent the dog jumping on to your lap.
- **Push the dog off.**
- Move to another area of the house.

**8. Praise and rewards should occur:**
- Within ten seconds of the dog's action.
- Within a minute or so.
- **Within two seconds of the dog's action.**
- Within 20 seconds of the dog's action.

**9. What is the most sensitive socialisation period of a dog's life?**
- 1–8 weeks.
- **5–16 weeks.**
- 12–20 weeks.
- 16–24 weeks.

**10. If a dog barks excessively for your attention when alone in a room, you should:**
- Wait ten minutes before entering the room.
- **Wait for a gap in the barking before entering the room.**
- Open the door quickly and throw the dog some food.
- Wait outside the room and reassure the dog with a soft voice.

# ACKNOWLEDGEMENTS

There are a few names without whom this book would not have been possible.

Firstly, many thanks to my long-suffering wife without whose patience and input you would not be reading this book. Not only was she a proofreader and ideas person, but also a calmer of emotions on days when senior moments prevented any thoughts from being formulated.

A very special thanks to two other people. First, to zoologist Dr Collette Coll, my colleague and source of information, for her many helpful and constructive comments. Also a huge thanks to Dr Amelia Welham BVSc BSc (Hons) MRCVS and Clinical Director at Vets-4Pets Bristol Imperial. Amelia reviewed the book from a veterinarian perspective.

And finally, thanks to Frank, whose mischievous and cheeky personality caused my daughter to raise a stream of questions about how to help him understand what was required of him in his new human home. It dawned on me that there must be millions of people in a similar situation to my daughter who would benefit from what I had to tell her. So, thank you, Frank, for inspiring me to write this book. Life is certainly duller when you're not around, albeit less stressful.

*Frank – copy-editing the book.*

# BIBLIOGRAPHY

The content of this book is based on and supported by research and over 20 years of experience. Set out below are some sources of supporting research.

Aloff, B. (2005) *Canine Body Language: A Photographic Guide: Interpreting the Native Language of the Domestic Dog.* Wenatchee, WA: Dogwise Publishing.

Ballamwar, V. A., Bonde, S. W., Mangle, N. S. and Vyavahare, S. H. (2008) 'Noise Phobia in Dogs.' *Veterinary World*, vol.1(11): 351–352.

Brice, D. (2021) 'Institute of Modern Dog Trainers – Behaviour, Understanding and Working With Canine Behaviour: Analysis and Application.'

Brice, D. (2020) Case webinar session.

Burch, M. R., and Bailey, J. S. (1999) *How Dogs Learn.* New York: Macmillan.

Bekoff, M. (2017) 'A Hierarchy of Dog Needs: Abraham Maslow Meets the Mutts.' *Psychology Today*. Available from https://www.psychologytoday.com/gb/blog/animal-emotions/201705/hierarchy-dog-needs-abraham-maslow-meets-the-mutts

Bekoff, M. (2002) *Minding Animals: Awareness, Emotions, and Heart*. New York: Oxford University Press.

Coppinger, R. and Coppinger, L. (2001) *Dogs: A Startling New Understanding of Canine Origin, Behaviour and Evolution*. New York: Scribner.

Eaton, B. (2008) *Dominance in Dogs: Fact or Fiction*. Wenatchee, WA: Dogwise Publishing.

Feldman Barrett, L. (2017) *How Emotions Are Made: The Secret Life of the Brain.* New York: Houghton Mifflin Harcourt.

Friedman, S. G. (2010) 'What's Wrong With This Picture? Effectiveness Is Not Enough.' *APDT Journal*, March/April 2010. Available from http://www.behaviorworks.org/files/articles/APDT%20 What%27s%20Wrong%20with%20this%20Picture%20-%20Dogs. pdf

Gagliano, M., Vyazovskiy, V., Borbély, A., Grimonprez, M. and Depczynski, M. (2016) 'Learning by Association in Plants.' *Scientific Reports* 6, 38427. Available from https://www.nature.com/articles/srep38427

Gaultier, E., Bonnafous, L., Bougrat, L., Lafont, C. and Pageat, P. 'Comparison of the efficacy of a synthetic dog-appeasing pheromone with clomipramine for the treatment of separation-related disorders in dogs.' *Vet Rec*, 156 (17):533–538. Available from https://pubmed. ncbi.nlm.nih.gov/15849342/

Gray, J. A. (1971) *The Psychology of Fear and Stress.* New York: McGraw Hill.

Heijnen, S., Hommel, B., Kibele, A. and Colzato, L. S. (2016) 'Neuromodulation of Aerobic Exercise – A Review.' *Frontiers in Psychology* 6:1890. doi: 10.3389/fpsyg.2015.01890

Hendriksen, P., Elmgreen, K. and Ladewig, J. (2011) 'Trailer-loading of horses: Is there a difference between positive and negative reinforcement concerning effectiveness and stress-related signs?' *Journal of Veterinary Behaviour*, vol. 6(5): 261–266. doi: 10.1016/j. jveb.2011.02.007

Horowitz, A. (2010) *Inside of a Dog: What Dogs See, Smell, and Know.* New York: Scribner.

Horwitz, D. F. and Mills, D. S. (eds.) (2010) *BSAVA Manual of Canine and Feline Behavioural Medicine,* 2nd ed. Gloucester: BSAVA.

Jacobs, J. A., Coe, J. B., Widowski, T. M., Pearl, D. L. and Niel, L. (2018) 'Defining and Clarifying the Terms Canine Possessive Aggression and Resource Guarding: A Study of Expert Opinion.' *Frontiers in Veterinary Science*, vol. 5. doi: 10.3389/fvets.2018.00115

Kaminski, J., Call, J. and Fischer, J. (2004) 'Word Learning in a Domestic Dog: Evidence for "Fast Mapping".' *Science*, vol. 304(5677):1682–3. doi: 10.1126/science.1097859

Landsberg, G. M. (2014) 'Diagnosis of Behavioural Problems.' *MSD Manual Veterinary Manual*.

Landsberg, G. M., Melese, P., Sherman, B. L., Neilson, J. C., Zimmerman, A. and Clarke, T. P. (2008) 'Effectiveness of fluoxetine chewable tablets in the treatment of canine separation anxiety.' *Journal of Veterinary Behaviour*, vol. 3(1):12–19.

Lindsay, S. R. (2005) *Handbook of Applied Dog Behaviour and Training: Volume Three, Procedures and Protocols*. Ames, IA: Blackwell Publishing.

McConnell, P. (2013) 'Resource Guarding: Treatment and Prevention.' *The Other End of the Leash*. Available from https://www.patriciamcconnell.com/theotherendoftheleash/resource-guarding-treatment-and-prevention

Mills, D., Dube, M. B. and Zulch, H. (2012) *Stress and Pheromonatherapy in Small Animal Clinical Behaviour*. Chichester: John Wiley & Sons.

Mills, D. (2005) 'Management of noise fears and phobias in pets.' *In Practice*, 27: 248– 255. Available from https://www.researchgate.net/profile/Daniel-Mills-3/publication/241844453_Management_of_noise_fears_and_phobias_in_pets/links/00b7d53b27c4f45603000000/Management-of-noise-fears-and-phobias-in-pets.pdf

Mobbs, D., Adolphs, R., Fanselow, M. S., Feldman Barrett, L., LeDoux, J. E., Ressler, K. and Tye, K. M. (2019) 'On the Nature of Fear.' *Scientific American*. Available from https://www.scientificamerican.com/article/on-the-nature-of-fear/

Moberg, G. P. and Mench, J. A. (2000) *The Biology of Animal Stress – Basic Principles and Implications for Animal Welfare*. Wallingford: CABI Publishing.

Mueller, S. (2020) *Hunting Together: Harnessing Predatory Chasing in Family Dogs through Motivation-Based Training*. Independently published.

O'Farrell, V. and Peachy, E. (1990). 'Behavioural effects of ovari-ohysterectomy on bitches.' *Journal of Small Animal Practice*, 31: 595–598. https://doi.org/10.1111/j.1748-5827.1990.tb00701

Ogata, N. and Dodman, N. H. (2011) 'The use of clonidine in the treatment of fear-based behavior problems in dogs: An open trial.' *Journal of Veterinary Behaviour*, vol. 6(2):130–137.

O'Heare, J. (2017) *Aggressive Behavior in Dogs, 3rd Edition*. Ottawa: Behave Tech Publishing.

Overall, K. L. (2013) *Manual of Clinical Behavioral Medicine for Dogs and Cats*. St. Louis, MO: Mosby.

Panksepp, J. and Biven, L. (2012) *The Archaeology of Mind: Neuroevolutionary Origins of Human Emotions*. New York, NY: W.W Norton & Company.

Panksepp, J. (2010) 'Affective neuroscience of the emotional Brain-Mind: evolutionary perspectives and implications for understanding depression.' *Dialogues in Clinical Neuroscience*, vol. 12(4): 533–545 doi: 10.31887/DCNS.2010.12.4/jpanksepp

Petersson, M., Uvnäs-Moberg, K., Nilsson, A., Gustafson, L., Hydbring-Sandberg, E. and Handlin, L. (2017) 'Oxytocin and Cortisol Levels in Dog Owners and Their Dogs Are Associated with Behavioral Patterns: An Exploratory Study.' *Frontiers in Psychology*, vol. 8. doi: 10.3389/fpsyg.2017.01796

Powdrill-Wells, N., Taylor, S. and Melfi, V. (2021) 'Reducing Dog Relinquishment to Rescue Centres Due to Behaviour Problems: Identifying Cases to Target with an Advice Intervention at the Point of Relinquishment Request.' *Animals*, vol. 11(10): 2766. doi:10.3390/ani11102766

Rigterink, A. and Houpt, K. (2014) 'Genetics of canine behavior: A review.' *World J Med Genet*, vol. 4(3): 46–57. doi: 10.5496/wjmg.v4.i3.46

Ryan, D. (2009) 'How do I stop my dog chasing?' *David Ryan: Dog Behaviour Author*. Available from https://www.dog-secrets.co.uk/how-do-i-stop-my-dog-chasing/

Sapolsky, R. M. (2017) *Behave: The Biology of Humans at Our Best and Worst*. London: Penguin.

Scott, J. P. and Fuller, J. L. (1998) *Genetics and the Social Behaviour of the Dog*. Chicago: University of Chicago Press.

Sharpe, M. J. (2018) 'What a relief! A role for dopamine in positive (but not negative) valence.' *Neuropsychopharmacology*, vol. 43: 1–2. Available from https://doi.org/10.1038/s41386-018-0036-6

Tenzin-Dolma, L. (2019) *The International School for Canine Psychology and Behaviour Diploma Course Textbook, 7th Edition*. UK: Phoenix Rising Press.

van der Borg, J. A. M., Matthijs, B. H. S., Vinke, C. M. and de Vries, H. (2015) 'Dominance in Domestic Dogs: A Quantitative Analysis of Its Behavioural Measures'. *PLoS ONE*, vol. 10 (8). Available from https://doi.org/10.1371/journal.pone.0133978

Vieira de Castro, A. C., Fuchs, D., Pastur, S., Munhoz-Morello, G., de Sousa, L. and Olsson, I. A. S. (2020) 'Does training method matter? Evidence for the negative impact of aversive-based methods on companion dog welfare.' *PLoS ONE*, vol. 15(12): e0225023 10.1371/journal.pone.0225023

Vieira de Castro, A. C., Barrett, J., de Sousa, L. and Olsson, I. A. S. (2019) 'Carrots versus sticks: The relationship between training methods and dog-owner attachment.' *Applied Animal Behaviour Science*, vol. 219: 104831 10.1016/j.applanim.2019.104831

Vieira de Castro, A. C., Araújo, A., Fonseca, A. and Olsson, I. A. S. (2021) 'Improving dog training methods: Efficacy and efficiency of reward and mixed training methods.' *PLoS ONE*, vol. 16(2): e0247321. doi: 10.1371/journal.pone.0247321

# INDEX

# AUTHOR PROFILE

Aftab Ahmed has worked with all dog breeds, ranging from Chihuahuas to Dobermans. He has dealt with virtually all unwanted behaviours our canine friends may exhibit and has particular expertise in working with rescue dogs, gun dogs, ridgebacks and companion dogs.

Aftab is a qualified dog behaviour consultant and dog trainer. He is accredited by several recognised organisations, including the International Association of Animal Behaviour Consultants (**IAABC**), the Institute of Modern Dog Trainers (**IMDT**), the International School of Canine Psychology & Behaviour (**ISCP**), the Guild of Dog Trainers (**GoDT**) and the Dog Training College (**DTC**).

In addition to helping owners with troublesome dog behaviours across England, Aftab delivers dog behaviour seminars both in England and abroad and has mentored dog behaviour students.

Aftab studied law at Southampton University and retired early from his successful legal career to take up dog behavioural work. He lives with his family and dogs in Esher, Surrey.

### What Did You Think of *To Be Frank Everything You Need to Know About Dog Behaviour?*

*A big thank you for purchasing this book. It means a lot that you chose this book specifically from such a wide range on offer. I do hope you enjoyed it.*

*Book reviews are incredibly important for an author. All feedback helps them improve their writing for future projects and for developing this edition. If you are able to spare a few minutes to post a review on Amazon, that would be much appreciated.*

## Publisher Information

Rowanvale Books provides publishing services to independent authors, writers and poets all over the globe. We deliver a personal, honest and efficient service that allows authors to see their work published, while remaining in control of the process and retaining their creativity. By making publishing services available to authors in a cost-effective and ethical way, we at Rowanvale Books hope to ensure that the local, national and international community benefits from a steady stream of good quality literature.

For more information about us, our authors or our publications, please get in touch.

www.rowanvalebooks.com
info@rowanvalebooks.com

Milton Keynes UK
Ingram Content Group UK Ltd.
UKHW052211040224
437145UK00001B/3

9 781914 422805